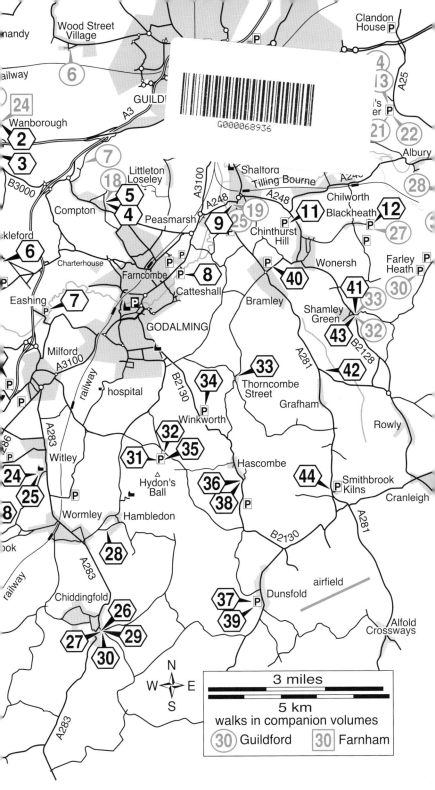

1 **Puttenham Common to the Hogs Back**

About 7.7 km/4¾ miles. Allow time for confusion on Puttenham Common.
Undulating farmland and heath; good in winter; soft sand in summer.
OS maps 1:25000 145 Guildford, 1:50000 186 Aldershot.

Start at Puttenham Common Top car park, SU 920 461,
or the roadside in the village, SU 930 478.

Linking walks 2❖ 3◇ 6✳ 13✦ 21❀ 22✳ 24❖

Harvester (Jolly Farmer) ☎ 01483 810374
The Good Intent ☎ 01483 810387

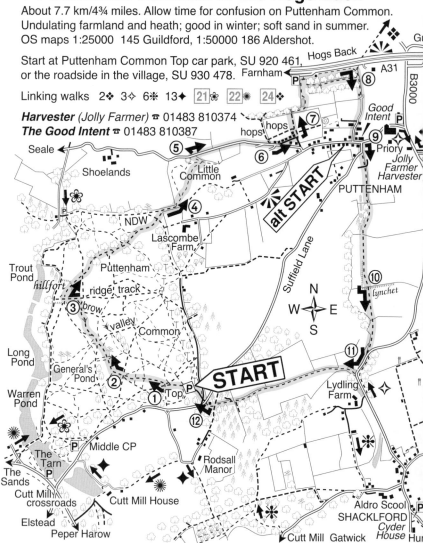

❀① At the corner of the car park opposite the access, go down the steep path (120m). Turn R on the cross path at the bottom. Cross the little valley and keep on round the hillside to the straight sloping cross path where other paths join (300m).
② Go straight on over a rise, down into a dip with several side paths (300m), up past a L fork (50m) to the brow (200m) ⬈ and L a bit to the straight level ridge path (100m)
③ Turn L on the path through the ramparts of the hill fort (100m) and take the first side path back R soon descending (200m). Cross a downhill path obliquely to the dip (100m). Disregard side paths and stay ahead up to the converging path (250m). Follow this into the deep

2

p, up again and over the curving erimeter path (350m) into the orner of the Common (80m).

④ Continue on the North Downs Way between fields (100m). Turn L n the side path immediately after ne L field and undulate obliquely own through the bracken (tall in ate summer) of Little Common 400m). Outside the next field, turn own L to the road below (50m).

⑤ Follow the road R (600m).

⑥ Bear L along Dark Lane (150m). Enter the hop garden at the bend.

⑦ Go L up the middle (150m). Climb the malmstone bank and turn R to the next field (80m). Go up the L edge round the pit in the trees to he top of the field (250m). Go R. ❖ Either get into the Hogs Back car park and walk along the A31 verge o the path R (350m) or go round he top of the field to the wood and cross it to the next field (100m). Walk along the top edge (200m).

⑧ Turn R straight down the path between hedges which becomes a track, then School Lane, to the village street in Puttenham (500m). Turn L to the ***Good Intent*** (50m). ◈

⑨ Opposite the pub, walk along Suffield Lane to the bend near the gate of Puttenham Priory (70m). Take the footpath ahead between fields (350m), past trees (200m) and on along above the bank (lynchet) in the next field (350m).

⑩ Near the corner of the lynchet drop to the next field and go on to the exit hidden under the brow of the hill (200m). Descend the short steep slope and continue round R to the road (250m).

⑪ Don't climb the bank opposite. Go down the road R to the L curve (130m) ✳ and R on the path in the trees. Continue around the L edge (lynchet) to the field (150m) and up the R edge to the end of the fields (550m). Stay ahead in the trees to the sunken bridleway (300m). ✦✳

⑫ Slightly L (10m), go up the other side and past a garden to the road, opposite Top car park (150m).

Hops

Hops are used in beer-brewing. They are cone-like flower heads of female plants. When picked they are sticky with resins and oils which give aroma and bitterness. Their use developed in the Low Countries in the middle ages when they were added to ale probably as a preservative at first. Wild hops, *Humulus lupulus*, are hedge climbers. About 30 cultvated varieties are grown in Britain - Fuggles at Puttenham.

A Mr Bignell brought hops to Farnham in 1597. In 1870 there were 72,000 acres in 53 counties as far north as Aberdeen. By 1995 this had shrunk to 7630 acres - 146 in Hampshire on three farms between Bentley and Worldham. By 2004 hop-growing had ceased in Hampshire. Converted hop kilns show where hops were grown.

The 12acre/5ha field below the Hogs Back at Puttenham was the last hop garden in Surrey. In March stringers are at work. Coir twine is used. It is looped round hooks on the cables and on the ground. In May, twiddlers train two shoots (bines) around each string and prune the surplus. In September the bines are cut out on their strings and carted to the picking machine and drier. The yield is about 30 zentners per acre after drying. 1 zentner=50kg.

Half of English hops become pellets, vacuum-packed and cooled. A quarter are used for hop extract, eluted with liquid carbon dioxide. The rest are used whole in traditional hopping.

2 Wanborough and Greyfriars Vineyard

About 7.4 km/4²/₃ miles with a short cut of 1.4 km/1 mile. Farmland and vineyard, long views, good all year; hilly, several stiles and two irksome crossings of the Hogs Back. OS maps 1:25000 145 Guildford, 1:50000 186 Aldershot.

Start from Wanborough beside the Great Barn, SU 934 488.

Linking walks   1❖   3✳   4✪
⑤ ✳   ⑦ ★   ⑱ ✳   23 ❖   24 ❀

Watts Gallery *Tea Shop* ☎ 01483 813590
Watts Gallery ☎ 01483 810235

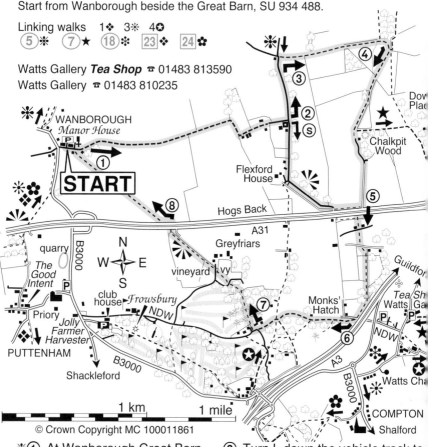

© Crown Copyright MC 100011861

✳① At Wanborough Great Barn, follow the track away from the road past the manor house, church and trees L (100m). Keep on between fields (1100m), round R & L bends and past barns to the T-junction at the East Flexford houses (500m).

Ⓢ *Short cut of 1.4 km/1 mile: Go up the track R (City of London visible far L) to the top of the Hogs Back (800m). Turn L along the verge of the A31 to the drive of Chalkpit Cottages (200m).*➔⑤

② Turn L down the vehicle track to the junction after the house (400m).

③ Turn R on the bridleway under trees between fields, eventually into a field (450m). Follow the L edge and go round the end, R of the wood, to the path junction at the bend in the hedge (250m).

④ Take the oblique track R up the middle of the field to trees (200m). Keep on at the L edge to the side path at the corner of Chalkpit Wood (300m). ★ The right-of-way is over ough ground to the cottages but walkers tend to keep to the edge of the field to the gate. Go up the drive onto the Hogs Back (500m).

⑤ Cross the A31 dual carriageway and turn R to the gate L (30m). Go straight down the field, over a track and a terrace then slightly L to the tarmac lane (200m). Cross to the opposite field and follow the path down the edge and along the bottom past a knoll with trees (300m). Continue along the foot of the A3 embankment to the drive (NDW) and gateway of Monks Hatch (200m). ✤✿◗✸

⑥ Cross the tarmac to the parallel North Downs Way path R. Follow it past side paths L and a cross path (550m) and join the vehicle track opposite houses (150m).

⑦ Ahead is Monks Grove Farm R (30m) ✤ Turn R on the path beside the drive. Pass between the houses and go straight up the hill, across two golf fairways and belts of pines then the path up the wood (300m). After the wood, bear L through scrub and over the farm track (100m). Keep on obliquely across Greyfriars Vineyard (100m) and over a track into the next part of the vineyard. Go up the R edge ↘↗ to the top of the Hogs Back (400m).

⑧ Cross the A31 dual carriageway then turn L (20m). Bear R down the footpath (old carriage road) to Wanborough church (800m). ✸

The Hogs Back has the most contorted strata of the North Downs chalk ridge. The chalk was once continuous over most of Britain. Here, it has become an anticline with the middle eaten out by erosion. The broken edges are the North and South Downs. Northwards the chalk dips under the London Basin to re-emerge as the Chiltern Hills.

The field track from Wanborough runs along the edge of the Chalk next to the London Clay on which cereals grow. Water from the chalk leaks out above the clay as a stream which would have attracted early settlers to Wanborough. The wooded hills seen to the north are the escarpment of the Tertiary Bagshot Sands plateau with infertile heath to Bracknell. It resists erosion because of a cap of flint gravel washed out from the chalk dome by Ice Age torrents.

Melbourne Rock, a hard layer in the Chalk, was quarried at Puttenham and used for the pillars of Compton Church. The Upper Greensand under the Chalk permits the hops to grow at Puttenham and yields the white malmstone of the hop kilns opposite the church. Gault clay accounts for the dry valley below the ridge because it allows the edge of the chalk to be undermined by erosion. It provided the clay for the terracotta tiles of the Watts chapel. The Folkstone Beds, top stratum of the Lower Greensand, are unlithified sands lacking calcium which cause the heath on Puttenham golf course and Puttenham Common.

3 Puttenham and Shackleford

About 9.0 km/5½ miles with a bluebell extension of 1.2 km/¾ mile through Compton. Good throughout the year; farmland and golf courses with long views; one short steep hill; one nasty road crossing and the hazards of golf. OS maps 1:25000 145 Guildford, 1:50000 186 Aldershot.

Start from the lay-by, SU 934 479, on the B3000 at the Puttenham side road or from Shackleford village car park in the road fork, SU 935 453.

Linking walks   1✧   2❋   4✿   5✿   6★   ⑱✿   ㉓❋   ㉔❋

The Harvester *(Jolly Farmer)* ☎ 01483 810374
The Good Intent ☎ 01483 810387
The Harrow ☎ 01483 810594
The Cyder House ☎ 01483 810360
The Squirrel Inn ☎ 01483 860223

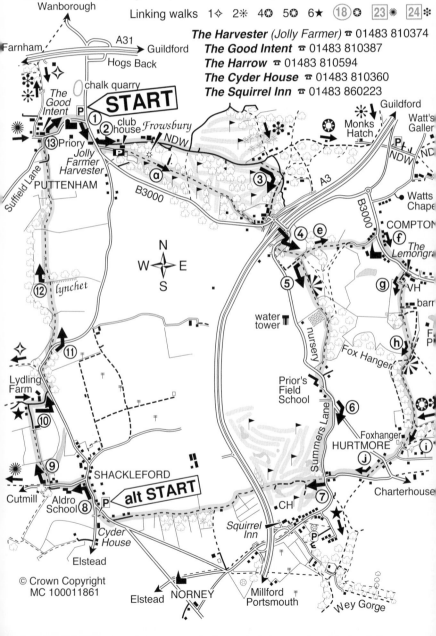

© Crown Copyright
MC 100011861

① From the Puttenham side road walk down the B3000 pavement to the **Harvester** (100m) then cross the road to the side track L (NDW).

ⓐ *Alternative: Follow waymarks along the golf course to Frowsbury (350m) and ahead (1100). Turn L along the road (150m).* ♦④

② Follow the NDW past Clear Barn (400m) and a side track L (300m), to houses L (500m). ✪

③ Opposite the 2nd cottage take the path R obliquely over the golf course into the trees, disregarding golf paths (150m). On the vehicle track turn R to the first house (50m) then fork R up to the next buildings (300m). Go L up to the roundabout.

④ Cross the A3 bridge (150m) and go R (Charterhouse)(150m). At the bend, opposite the first drive, turn L up the fields to the cross path in the trees on top (250m).

ⓔ *Extension of 1¼ km/¾ mile via Compton: Turn L down the path and continue along the lane to the B3000 in Compton (600m).*

ⓕ *Follow the pavements R down to the **Harrow** R (300m).*

ⓖ *Go down the drive beside the pub (70m) and L to fields (50m). Follow the R hedge over the rise (200m) and go straight on across the field to the cart track (200m).*

ⓗ *Turn R up to the corner of the wood (50m) and carry on round the undulating R edge of the field below Fox Hanger (350m).*

ⓘ *Just before the corner, exit R on the uphill path (150m). Stay ahead on the drive to the road in Hurtmore (150m) and the track opposite to the next road (150m).*★

ⓙ *Go R down the road to the bend at Summer's Lane (300m).* ♦⑦

⑤ Turn R and, almost immediately, L into the flat field. Follow the L edge (of the Bargate escarpment) past the water tower far R (350m) to the road opposite Prior's Field School (450m). Continue along the road L (250m).

⑥ Go R down Summers Lane to the road junction (500m). ★

⑦ Take the path straight across the golf course: faint path then vehicle track then faint path, to the A3 (500m). Cross the dual carriageway. Stay ahead on the path, round a L bend (100m) and, past a side path (250m) to the road (700m). Cross the road to the path up the bank and turn R to the road junction (150m). (**Cyder House** L).

⑧ From the car park walk through Shackleford (200m) and take the Cutmill side road L to the footpath beside the last house R (250m). ✸

⑨ Go R along the bottom edge of the fields. Stay ahead past houses to the wall of Lydling Farm (550m).

⑩ Turn R on the drive down to the road at the pond (200m). ✦ Cross to the path on the opposite bank and follow it L in the trees above the road to its end (300m).

⑪ Cross into the field opposite and follow the L edge up the short steep slope under trees into the next field (250m). Over the brow bear slightly R and climb the bank (lynchet) into the next field (200m).

⑫ Stay ahead on the path along the L edge and all the way to Puttenham (see Puttenham Priory R) (900m) then along Suffield Lane to the **Good Intent** (70m). ✸✸

⑬ Turn R up the road past the church and converted hop kilns L to the B3000 and lay-by (400m).

4 Compton and Binscombe

About 7.8 km/4¾ miles with an extension of 700 m/½ mile. Farmland and woods, bluebells in season. OS maps 1:25000 145 Guildford, 1:50000 186 Aldershot.

Start from the roadside opposite the *Withies* in Withies Lane at Compton, SU 963 468, or outside Watts Gallery or the Watts Chapel.

Linking walks   2✿   3✿   5✳   6♣   ⑦✳   ⑱✿   24✡

The Harrow ☎ 01483 810594   **The Withies** ☎ 01483 421158
Watts Gallery **Tea Shop** ☎ 01483 813590   Watts Gallery ☎ 01483 810235

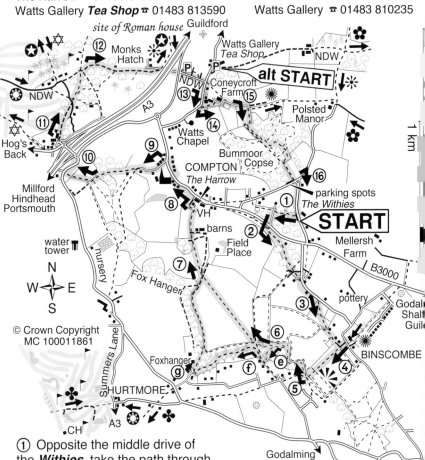

① Opposite the middle drive of the **Withies**, take the path through the trees on Compton Common to the first house drive (150m).

② Turn L to the road and cross to the tarmac path behind the trees (100m). Follow this path L, round to the next road (500m). Carry on ahead along the road (R) to the first field R (200m).

③ Cross the fields obliquely to the hedge at the top corner (200m). Outside, go L along the path to the houses (150m). Turn L to the road to see old Binscombe (50m).

④ Return between the houses (50m) and go straight up the field to the wood (300m).

⑤ Before the trees look back. ↘↗

The large house beyond Binscombe is Loseley Park. The Hogs Back is L. The cluster of radio masts is above Guildford which is hidden in the notch where the River Wey cuts the North Downs ridge. Gleaming white at the high point is Semaphore House. The ridge disappears behind Chantries Hill with St Martha's as the bump on the end. The sharp green spire in front of Chantries is Shalford Church. Slightly L of it is the solitary mast at the Mount Browne Surrey Police HQ. The distant asymmetric hill R is Leith Hill.

Continue into the trees (10m). Turn R and immediately branch R on the small path undulating and winding near the foot of the wood (250m). At the gully, descend a bit (40m), then climb the L bank and take the L path to a fork: up L/down R (80m).

ⓔ *Extension of 700m/½ mile: Fork L steeply up past gardens on the Bargate sandstone plateau (150m).*

ⓕ *Turn R on the larger path from between the gardens (100m) then diverge L on the path up through the coppice above the escarpment to the drive at the end (500m).* ✪

ⓖ *Turn back R down the path below the house (200m). Enter the field and go L round the undulating top edge, below Fox Hanger (500m). At the end of the wood carry on down (50m) towards the large house, Field Place. At the side track halfway down, turn into the L field.* ➔⑦

⑥ Fork R. Continue in the trees to the path junction at the foot of steps (150m). Enter the corner of the field R and cross obliquely, down, up. Aim for the end of the wood beyond the ridge (550m). At the track cross into the next field.

⑦ Take the path diverging L of the track to the hedge L of the barns (300m). At the bottom turn L (50m) and R to the **Harrow** (70m).

⑧ Walk up the village street L through Compton, past White Hart Cottage and Eastbury Manor (200m). Visit the church then go on up the pavement opposite (100m).

⑨ Cross to Eastbury Lane L. Walk to the end of the lane (250m) and fork R up the sandy hillside path to the side path R on top (350m).

⑩ Go down through fields to the road (200m). Follow the pavement down R (150m). Cross the roundabout to walk over the A3 bridge on the R pavement (120m).

⑪ Continue ahead to the garage (50m) then take the path R into the wood. ✪ Stay ahead, over the cart track obliquely, near houses R (300m), to the 4-way junction at the North Downs Way (250m).

⑫ Go R on the NDW to the Monks' Hatch road bridges (600m). ❋ Follow the tarmac (NDW) under the bridges to the road (400m). ❀ (Watts Gallery **Tea Shop** L 100m).

⑬ Follow the road R to the end of the Coneycroft Farm buildings (200m). *If visiting Watts Chapel keep on along the lane (200m) and up into the cemetery, then return.*

⑭ Take the path zigzagging R of the farm buildings and go along the straight concrete track (400m). ❋

⑮ At the end fence, turn R on the path which skirts the field into the wood (200m). It is better to use the unofficial paths L of the RoW, with a bulge to the L (400m) then rejoin the RoW to Polsted Lane (150m).

⑯ Slightly L (10m) continue on the road ahead to the **Withies** (200m).

5 Binscombe and Loseley Park

About 8.3 km/5¼ miles with an extension of 1.2 km/¾ mile to Watts Gallery. Farm country and bluebell woods. In summer Loseley Park can be visited *en route*. OS maps 1:25000 145 Guildford, 1:50000 186 Aldershot.

Start from Compton. Park at the roadside opposite *The Withies*, SU 963 468.

Linking walks   3✿   4✳   ⑦❖   ⑱✳   ⑲◇   24✳

The Withies ☎ 01483 421158   **The Harrow** ☎ 01483 810594
Watts Gallery **Tea Shop** ☎ 01483 8133590   Watts Gallery ☎ 01483 810235
Loseley House ☎ 01483 304440

① At the **Withies**, walk away from the main road to the end of the lane (200m). Cross Polsted Lane and, slightly L, take the path at the edge of the wood (200m). Turn R on the 1st side path in the wood. Curve back towards the main path and carry on R of it to the end of the wood (500m). Skirt round the fields to the path R just before the concrete farm track (200m). ❖

ⓔ *Extension of 1 km/¾ mile to Watts Gallery: Go L on the concrete farm track (200m), R up the side path at the start of the buildings (150m) and R on the road (100m).*

Return along the road to the end of the farm buildings L (200m).

⑦ *Turn L on the path zigzagging R of the buildings. Keep on to the end of the concrete track (400m).*

⑧ Take the footpath away from the farm outside the hillside field, ultimately past a garden R and down steps to the deep sunken path (600m). ✳

③ Turn R down to the lane near Polsted Manor (30m) and L up the track that continues from the lane. Keep on past a house L (400m) to the Loseley Park gateway (300m).

④ Take the path L at the boundary (200m). The path bends R at the bottom edge of the fields, crosses a farm track and passes the pond (400m). Loseley Park is visible R. Keep on over the fields, rising slightly L, to the road at Pillarbox Cottage in Littleton (500m).✧

⑤ Go R on the road down through the village and over a rise (600m).

⑥ Turn R on the tarmac Loseley drive to the first house L (300m).

⑦ Turn L into the field next to the house (50m). Cross the R corner (100m) and the next field on the same oblique line to the drive outside, not at the gateway but 70m before the bottom corner, (400m).

⑧ Turn L on the drive. Watch out for the path R into the trees opposite the track from the next L field (80m). Go through to the field and along the ditch (150m). Stay ahead to the cross hedge (150m).

⑨ Turn L beside the hedge to the B3000 (200m). Cross the road (30m R) and go through the football field. The public footpath is parallel with the R end (100m). Cross the next road to the grass, slightly L,

and follow the path in the trees, R of the side road, to the road in Binscombe (450m).

⑩ Go L along the road (150m) and up the edge of the first field R to the top (300m). ↘

⑪ Follow the path R, round the top of the adjacent field, either in the field or through the trees above it (250m). Watch out for an upward path L, 30m before the next corner. Climb the stepped path (up the Bargate escarpment) to the flat top and pass between gardens (200m).

⑫ At the road bend, take the path R, between gardens (200m). Avoid side paths and continue to the descending steps. Drop down the escarpment to the path junction outside the corner of a field (100m). Don't enter the field but go down the path between the fields (300m), to the field below and round the R edge to the trees of Compton Common (300m). Stay ahead in the trees, over cross tracks, ultimately converging on the road (100m).

⑬ Turn L along the road (100m). Cross the B3000 and walk along the lane to the *Withies* (200m).

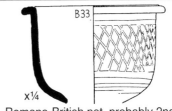

Romano-British pot, probably 2nd century, found with many other shards when the Binscombe Crescent houses were built in 1953. The site is thought to have been an ordinary homestead rather than a villa. The archæologist's sketch shows the section as well as surface.
+SAC v57 1960 *Romano-British Farms*

6 Shackleford, Eashing and Peper Harow

About 8.0 km/5 miles, with extensions of 400m/¼ mile and 800m/½ mile; fields and woods; soft sand and nettles in summer, little shade, gentle rises. OS maps 1:25000 145 Guildford, 1:50000 186 Aldershot.

Start at Shackleford car park in the road fork, SU 935 453, or from the little car park in Lower Eashing at the end of the bridges, SU 946 438.

Linking 1✳ 3★ 4♣ 7✦ 13✺ 26✳

The Cyder House ☎ 01483 810360
The Squirrel ☎ 01483 860223
The Stag ☎ 01483 421568

★① Behind Shackleford car park, follow the path L round the edge of the field next to the road (150m). Cross L into Rokers Lane. Go past the houses (150m) and on between fields L and trees R (550m). ♣

② Take the side path R, between fences. Keep on to the road (400m).

③ Turn L along the footpath L of the road to the A3 bridge (350m). Continue on the pavement to the slip road L from the A3 with access to the **Squirrel** (200m).

④ Just before the slip road, cross the road to the gate and take the path down L to the lane under the road or pass under from the **Squirrel** forecourt. Keep on down past houses R & L to the cross path at the rounded corner of the garden wall in the Wey Gorge (450m). ✦

⑤ Turn R on the curving bridleway up the valleyside past a side path R in the trees. Stay ahead over the rise (150m) then level to pillboxes (700m) and along the concrete farm track into Eashing (400m).

ⓧ *Extension of 800m/½mile into*
ashing: Go L, over the bridges
250m) and round the bend as far
s **The Stag** *(150m), then return.*

ⓧ Walk out of the village to the
3 (100m). Cross the bridge, up R,
ⓘ the field (150m) and go up round
ⓘe R edge to the exit under trees
t the 2nd corner (500m). Turn R.

ⓧ *Option: Keep straight on to the*
ⓘad (500m). Cross to Shackleford
ⓘommon and carry on to the next
ⓘad (300m). Cross and carry on
ⓘ00m). In the trees at the end of
ⓘe R field go round the L bend,
ⓘeside the boundary ditch to
ⓘarren Lodge (400m). Turn R. ➔⑩

ⓧ Immediately turn L through the
ⓘees (40m) and go straight over
ⓘe field parallel with the bottom
ⓘdge. <u>Park House</u> is visible L.
ⓘass L of the dovecote and barn to
ⓘe church at <u>Peper Harow</u> (350m).

ⓧ Go up the lane (50m). Step into
ⓘe yard R to see Home Farm then
ⓘarry on (250m). Round the bend
ⓘfter the gardens, enter the field L.
ⓘake for the far R corner (400m).

⑨ Cross the road into the field
and follow the track ahead to the
house, Warren Lodge (450m).

⑩ Follow the undulating drive to
the road (450m).

⑪ Go R on the road (100m). On
the R curve, soon after the L field,
turn L up the winding path into the
wood (300m). ❀ Keep on ahead
up to the 4-way junction (70m). ✱

ⓔ *Extension of 800m/½ mile:*
Take the track ahead, between
the wood L and fields R all the way
to Lydling Farmhouse L (1100m).

ⓕ *Backtrack (30m) and take the*
side track past Lydling Cottages to
the end (150m). Carry straight on
to the bottom of the fields and join
the road (400m). ➔⑬

⑫ Take the woodland track R to
the R bend (400m) then go down
the field ahead converging on the
R hedge to the bend halfway down
(200m). Drop to the road and go
down past the side path L (120m).

⑬ Continue into the village (250m)
and turn R to the car park (200m).
For the **Cyder House** fork R 100m.

Charterhouse School has spires that make it a distinctive landmark on many of the walks in this book but here is no public path or road which allows a close view. It is one of the ancient public schools. The name derives from its original position near Barts in London, on the site of a Carthusian monastery. Thomas Sutton bought the post-Dissolution property from the Duke of Norfolk in 1611 to build the school. It moved to Godalming in 1872 when the main building was completed. *Photo Adrian Furniss*

7 Eashing, the Wey Gorge and Godalming

About 8.1 km/5 miles with a short cut of 1¾ km/1 mile bypassing Godalming town centre. Good views in winter, few stiles, one steep slope, quite a lot of tarmac. OS maps 1:25000 145 Guildford, 1:50000 186 Aldershot.

Start in Lower Eashing, from the little car park at the west end of the bridges, SU 946 438, or in Godalming, at the long lay-by in Borough Road, SU 968 443.

Linking walks 6✦ 8✳

The King's Arms ☎ 01483 421545
The Red Lion ☎ 01483 428828
The Sun ☎ 01483 415505
The Stag ☎ 01483 421568
The Squirrel ☎ 01483 860223

✦① From Eashing bridges walk through the village towards the A3 (200m). Turn R on the tarmac drive before the last house and continue on the concrete farm track (400m). Stay ahead on the bridleway (650m) and round L into a side valley down to a tarmac lane outside a garden wall (150m).

ⓦ *Winter alternative on a higher path. Carry on R of the wall (80m) and turn R up the valley side (80m). Turn R along the path just below the brow of the gorge (650m).*

ⓧ *When level with the field, go R down the stepped side path (50m). Continue on the lower path (100m) and fork down R to the cross path (100m). Cross past the buildings R to the Charterhouse drive (80m).*

ⓨ *Descend (100m). Cross the road and go on down the footpath to the river (200m). Turn L.* ✦④

② Turn R on the lane round the bend in the valley (150m). Pass L the house on the path in the Wey gorge to Peperharow Road in Godalming (700m).

③ Turn R down the path beside the houses to the River Wey (150m) and go L along the bank (300m).

④ Continue along the tarmac path diverging L outside Westbrook Mill (600m). Cross the drive to Borough Road (50m). Turn R under the railway then use the footpath R of the wall and cross the river (200m).

Guildford
Squirrel
Puttenham
Shackleford
NORNEY
Elstead
school
Norney Farm
pb
pillbox
START
fb
LOWER EASHING mill *buhr* cliff
The Stag
UPPER EASHING
Eashing Farm

N
W ✦ E
S

© Crown Copyright
MC 100011861

B3001
Elstead
Farnham
Hindhead
Portsmouth
Milford

A3
A283

ⓢ *Short cut of 1¾ km/1 mile: Turn R on Vicarage Walk over the River Ock (100m). Follow the lane R up under the railway, past Westbrook Place (The Meath), to the top (600m). At the L bend. continue ahead on the drive past Shepherd Cottage (public footpath)(80m).* ✦⑩

14

⑤ Cross the road into the park. Go past the <u>Phillips Memorial</u> Cloisters and follow the riverside path (opposite the <u>Lammas Land</u>) to the next road (700m). ✳

ⓘ If you want to see the site of the wharf on the end of the <u>Godalming Navigation</u>:   Cross the road and river. Go round the wall R and along the river bank to the L bend (300m). Return to the road. Turn L.

⑥ Go up Bridge Street to the ***Sun***, (300m) and bear R past the ***King's Arms*** along High Street (350m).

⑦ After the Pepper-pot (50m) go R on the passageway next to the ***Red Lion***, over the road, down Mill Lane to Hatch Mill on the River Ock and up to the station (350m). Cross the station footbridge.

⑧ Join the drive behind the station and turn L to the houses (300m).

⑨ Go up round the bend in the drive and continue up the path under trees to the farm on top (400m). Carry on along the drive (or the edge of the R field) round the ½R bend to the sharp L bend near the cottage (200m).

⑩ Follow the level tarmac drive between flat fields above the Ock and Wey gorges (Charterhouse spires back R) to the road (900m).

⑪ Go R beside the road (250m), round the L bend at Upper Eashing and on (250m).

⑫ At the first house R turn into the field and go straight along the shoulder (edge of the burh) to the the end (250m). Descend L through the trees on the river bank to Eashing Bridges near the cliff (200m). The ***Stag*** is ahead (100m), beyond the offices (formerly <u>Eashing Mill</u>).

Charterhouse   Hog's Back
Puttenham
A3/B3000 junction
ⓨ
Peperharow Road
Portsmouth Line
④ **alt START**
Wey Gorge
Guildford
Westbrook   mill
Lammas Land   ⓘ
⑧   Ⓢ   ⑤   King's Arms   Sun   ⑥   wharf
Star
mill   High Street
⑨   ⑦ Red Lion
River Ock   GODALMING
A3100   Winkworth
Holloway Hill   Hascombe
Tuesley
ord   mill   Tuesley
B2130

...scingum is one of the 27 **burh**s listed in the "Burhal Hidage" of around 915, set up in Wessex to counter the Viking predations. Probably initiated by Alfred the Great, they were barracks, refuges mobilisation depots and strong points for militias to drive the Danes out of Wessex. For manning and sustenance they were apportioned parts of the kingdom. The 600 hides allocated to ...scingum indicate a garrison of 600 men. Four men were stipulated for each pole (5½ yards) of wall. These figures accord with the rectangle of land at Eashing between the river cliff and two dry side valleys (now marked by road and footpath), if the cliff were unmanned. The nearest burhs were at Southwark, Winchester, Chichester and Sashes Island on the Thames at Cookham. Why Eshing 'disappeared' is obscure. Many burhs became new towns (boroughs) as the defenders required markets and services. Extra burhs were built in Mercia when the non-Danish parts were absorbed by Alfred's son, Edward the Elder, and they were copied by the Franks.

8 Catteshall, Nurscombe and Navigation

About 7.7 km/4¾ miles with an extension of 2.6 km/1²/₃ mile. Best when the Navigation is active. Hilly; soft sand on the towpath in summer, boggy in wet seasons in (h). OS maps 1:25000 145 Guildford, 1:50000 186 Aldershot.

Start at the Manor Inn, SU 984 450. On the extension, use the car park at the E corner of Broad Water, SU 985 453.

Linking walks 7✱ 9✱ 28☆

Beefeater Manor Inn 01483 427134
The Leathern Bottle 01483 497632
Hector's on the Wey 01483 418769

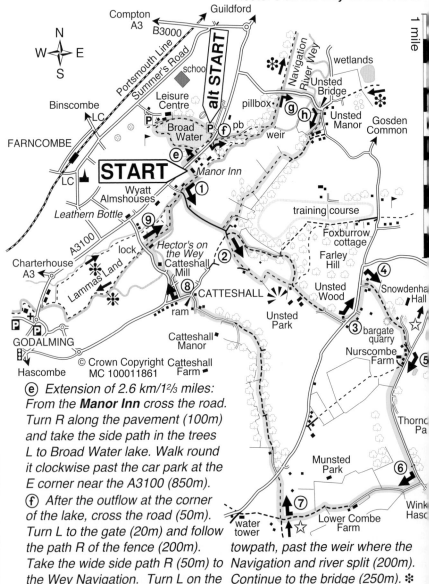

© Crown Copyright
MC 100011861

(e) *Extension of 2.6 km/1²/₃ miles:*
*From the **Manor Inn** cross the road. Turn R along the pavement (100m) and take the side path in the trees L to Broad Water lake. Walk round it clockwise past the car park at the E corner near the A3100 (850m).*
(f) *After the outflow at the corner of the lake, cross the road (50m). Turn L to the gate (20m) and follow the path R of the fence (200m). Take the wide side path R (50m) to the Wey Navigation. Turn L on the* towpath, past the weir where the Navigation and river split (200m). Continue to the bridge (250m). ✱

16

(g) Cross the Navigation, then the river, then Unsted Bridge on the L curve (look back at it) (350m).

(h) Turn R into Unsted Lane (20m) then cross the field R to the corner beyond the barn (150m). Exit to the track near houses (30m) and go R over a rise and down (250m). At the end of the track turn R then L on the fenced path along the fields. Keep on to the rising track after the house L (650m). Turn L. ➔②

① At the **Manor Inn** go through the garden to the Godalming Navigation. Turn R on the towpath to the bridge (150m). Cross and follow the track past the house L (400m).

② At the 4-way junction (35m), the path directly uphill (680m) is closed temporarily. Instead, go L up the winding bridleway, under trees. Ignore the two side paths L (700m). Go round a L bend near a house then straight, past the Unsted Park buildings R, over the top (200m) and down to the road (250m).

③ Go up the road L, over the top and halfway down (300m).

④ Enter the drive R of the house Wood End and take the path L of the garden. Carry on under trees down to the next road in Nurscombe (600m). ☆

⑤ Follow the road R (950m).

⑥ Just before the Thorncombe Park drive L, turn R up the tarmac drive of Lower Combe Farm (550m). Continue up the track R of the buildings then up the bridleway under trees (550m).

⑦ At the 4-way junction take the footpath down R between fences to the road (300m). Walk down the drive opposite. Keep on into the valley past the gates L of the farm (1200m) and Catteshall Manor to the bottom near the ram (400m).

⑧ Turn L along Catteshall Lane (80m) ✳ and R along Catteshall Road (120m). Walk through the residential part then join the main road past Catteshall Mill and over the Godalming Navigation bridge (300m). See the lock L. (The **Leathern Bottle** is 200m ahead).

⑨ R of the road is **Hector's on the Wey**. Take the towpath, past the Wyatt Almshouses L at the R curve (300m), to the next bridge (150m). Keep on to the garden of the Manor Inn (150m) and go through it.

Oak apples are green outgrowths that form in two weeks in May. A 5mm wasp, *Biorhiza pallida*, lays eggs in a bud, re-programming it to develop into the gall. These eggs are unfertilized but hatch into grubs, about 30 per gall. They emerge in July as 3mm wasps which mate and lay fertilized eggs on the roots, inducing 10mm hard root galls for over-wintering with one grub each. The females from these grubs lay eggs in buds again. Other species of gall wasp invade the gall, some (inquilines) to share it and others to parasitise the gall-makers.

Oak apples
actual size

9 Shalford, Gosden Common and Unsted

About 9 km/5²/₃ miles. The extension of 1.4 km/¾ mile over Chinthurst Hill and the short cut of 2.8 km/1¾ miles can be used together. Undulating, half shady, on the Greensand. OS maps 1:25000 145 Guildford, 1:50000 186 Aldershot.

Start at Shalford, parking on the side road in front of *The Parrot*, SU 998 468. Alternatively, on the extension, start at Chinthurst Hill car park, TQ 014 463.

Linking walks   8❋   10★   11◇
40♣   ⑲◉   ⑳❋   ㉕❀

The Parrot ☎ 01483 561400
The Queen Victoria ☎ 01483 566959
Grantley Arms ☎ 01483 893351

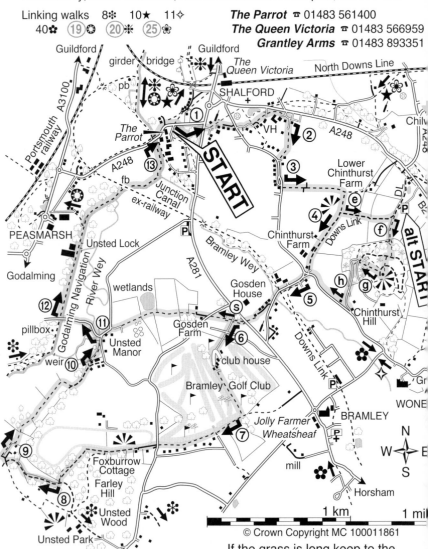

© Crown Copyright MC 100011861

❋① At the **Parrot** cross the grass (Shalford) Green in front of the pub, curving away from the A248 then back towards it at the top (200m).

If the grass is long keep to the pavement. At the junction with the Horsham road, A281, cross to the cricket pitch and skirt round the R edge of the main green, over

18

Chinthurst Lane (200m) and on, R of the pond (in bushes) (200m), to the corner of the green (200m).

② Pass Station Road L, Ashley House R and the next house then turn R on the drive. Continue on the footpath between gardens to the road (300m). Follow it L to the end of the first field L (200m).

③ Take the path L between the fields (450m). ✧ After the rise and the R curve, turn R on the side path between fields (150m).

ⓔ *Extension of 1.4 km/¾ miles: At the bridleway (Downs Link) go L to a T-junction (350m).(Car park L.)*

ⓕ *Turn R up* Chinthurst Hill. *Keep to uphill paths to the tower on top (450m). (*◣↗*see box Walk 11)*

ⓖ *From the back of the tower, opposite the doorway, descend the steepest path to the tarmac drive (200m) and go down it (350m).* ❀

ⓗ *At the road, descend R to the next junction (400m). Turn L.* ➔⑤

④ Stay ahead on the bridleway down to the road junction (500m).

⑤ Go down Tannery Lane (200m). Cross the Horsham Railway bridge (now route of the Downs Link path) and the Bramley Wey bridge to Gosden Common (100m). Turn off the road along the R edge of the green (see the plaque at the cricket pavilion) (200m). Cross the A281 and follow the R path to the tarmac golf club drive (100m).

ⓢ *Short cut of 2.8 km/1¾ miles: Stay ahead across the road (150m), along Gosden Farm drive (80m), between fields (wetlands R) (500m) and along the sewage works drive to the road (near Unsted Manor (70m). Turn L on the road, round the R bend (100m).* ❀ ➔⑪

⑥ Go L on the drive (100m), up the sloping car park (100m) and briefly up the drive between huts (50m). Branch off R on the public path skirting the brow of the hill to the far edge (350m).

⑦ Turn R on the boundary path to the end of the golf course (600m). Continue over the road up the Foxburrow drive and beside the wood, ◣↗ past the side path L

> Far R Guildford is visible in the notch where the River Wey cuts through the North Downs ridge between the Hogs Back and Pewley Down. Round R are St Martha's and Chinthurst Hills.

(350m), ❉ round a L bend (150m) into the wood and down steeply to the junction in the cleft (300m).

⑧ Turn R down beside the field to the vehicle track (400m) and go R down to the house drive (50m).

⑨ Just after the drive (20m) take the side path R (100m). Go round R & L bends and on between fields at the edge of the Wey flood-plain (600m), round R (100m) then L up the farm track (200m).

⑩ At the next house take the side path L to the field (30m) and follow the L edge to the lane (100m). Go L to the road (40m) and L again.

⑪ Step on to the R verge to see Unsted Bridge. Carry on across the River Wey and the Godalming Navigation bridges (300m).

⑫ Descend to the towpath R and follow it past Unsted Lock (500m), the Peasmarsh path L ✪ (100m), the bridge (old Horsham Railway) (350m) and the Junction Canal R (250m) to the A286 (250m). ❉

⑬ Cross to the pavement. Follow the road R, over the bridge and round to the *Parrot* (100m).

10 Shalford, Chantries and St Martha's Hill

About 7.6 km/4¾ miles with a short cut of 1.0 km/²/₃ mile. Steep slopes; soft sand in summer; long views; bluebells in season; good for winter walking.
OS maps 1:25000 145 Guildford, 1:50000 186 Aldershot.

Start from Chantries car park, Shalford, TQ 003 483 or from St Martha's Hill (Halfpenny Lane) car park, TQ 021 484. Two stations are near the route.

Linking walks 9★ ⑧✛ ⑫❂ ⑲☆ ⑳✪ ㉑✧ ㉕★ ㉖✿ ㉗❀

The Sea Horse ☎ 01483 514351   ***The Queen Victoria*** ☎ 01483 566959

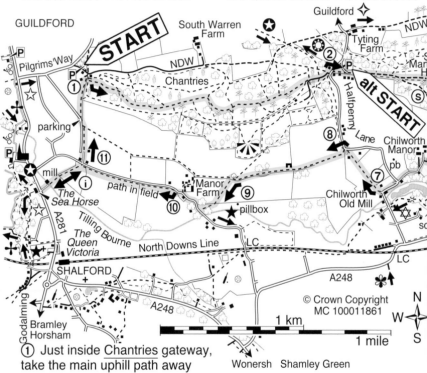

① Just inside <u>Chantries</u> gateway, take the main uphill path away from the fence (not the small path near the garden) onto the ridge.

↘ Watch out for the cathedral L. Keep on along the undulating and winding ridge-top always taking the highest onward path until you reach Halfpenny Lane (2000m). ❂

② Go L up the lane (50m) then R up the side path (NDW) past the car park L and houses R (50m). ✧ Keep on up <u>St Martha's Hill</u> on the wide sandy track and through the churchyard W gate (700m). ✿

ⓢ *Short cut of 1.0 km/²/₃ mile: From the S door of the church drop to the S gate and go down the very steep path to the end (500m).* ➔⑥

③ Leave the churchyard by the E gate and stay ahead on the main path over the ironstone outcrop and down the edge of the hill almost to the pillbox L (400m).

④ Turn back R down the broad track (Downs Link), soon between fields (300m). Go round the R bend and on to the L bend (150m).

⑤ Just round the L bend, turn up into the field above. Go over the bottom edge to the downhill path (300m). Descend L (150m).

⑥ At the bottom (150m) ❧ turn R on the track from the vineyard towards Chilworth Manor (50m) and L down the drive to Halfpenny Lane (350m). Stay ahead to the L bend at Blacksmith Lane (150m).

⑦ Bear R up the path above Old Mill to the road (400m).

⑧ Turn into the field L. Follow the track at the L edge (400m), past farm buildings R, over a rise and into a dip (400m).

⑨ After the hillside path back R (40m), take the ½L path over the field to the hedge and go down steps to the road near the Tilling (300m).★ Go R up the road (150m).

⑩ Just after the roadside house L ignore the field gate (30m). At the next gate (30m) enter the field L and follow the footpath beside the road hedge from field to field to the end near houses (600m). ✦⑪

ⓘ *If visiting the **Sea Horse** go down the field L and along the path past* Shalford Mill *(250m) to the road opposite the pub (50m).*☆✪✝ *Return the same way to the top.*

⑪ Exit from the field, cross the lane and follow the drive opposite. Stay ahead on the footpath then the road outside fields R (300m). At the ½L road bend, diverge R on the path over the foot of the hill to the Chantries car park at the North Downs Way (350m).

The entry for Shalford in the Surrey pages of the Domesday Book, 1086. TRE means before the Conquest, *Tempore Regis Edwardi,* in the time of King Edward. The line through SCALDEFOR was red for highlighting.

actual size

Robert holds SCALDEFOR from Richard. Two brothers held it TRE.
Each had his own house but they remained in one court.
They could go where they would. Then & now it rated for iiii hides. Land for vi ploughs. In demesne are ii ploughs; xxix villeins & xi bordars with ix ploughs. There is a church; x slaves. iii mills @ xvi shillings; iiii acres of pasture. Wood @ xx pigs. Of these hides one man-at-arms holds one virgate, where he has half a plough & i slave & v bordars.
Total value TRE xvi pounds; later ix pounds. Now xx pounds.
To this manor belongs one property in Guildford @ iii shillings.

11 Chinthurst Hill and Blackheath

About 7.9 km/5 miles. Greensand hills with good views; short steep slopes; soft sand when dry; slippery in winter; half shady. Allow time for confusion on the Blackheath paths. OS maps 1:25000 145 Guildford, 1:50000 186 Aldershot.

Start at Chinthurst Hill car park, TQ 014 462, or Blackheath village, TQ 036 462.

Linking walks   9✧   10✿   12★   40✦
(25)❖ (27)✪ (32)✱

Grantley Arms ☎ 01483 893351

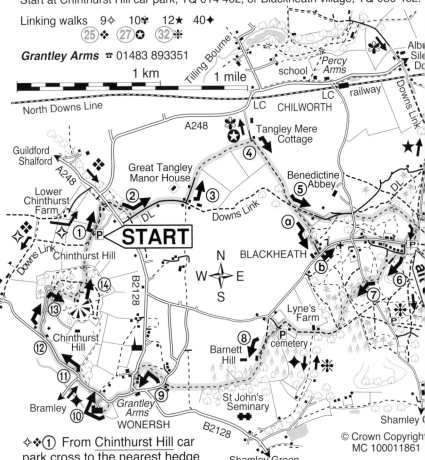

© Crown Copyright
MC 100011861

✧✿① From Chinthurst Hill car park cross to the nearest hedge and walk down the path behind it to the B2128 (200m).

② Cross to the path opposite. Follow it obliquely R (200m) and turn L along the lane past the drive of Great Tangley Manor House L (400m) to the 4-way junction of tracks and a path (100m).

③ Turn L past the buildings and go round the foot of the hill to the cottage at the end (700m). ✪✿

④ Turn R up the bridleway between the fields into the wood to the level track on top (500m).

ⓐ *Equal alternative through* Blackheath *village: Go straight on between fences (200m). After the R field, fork R through the trees and descend R of houses (200m).*

ⓑ *Walk up the road L past the church (100m) and crossroads (100m) to the car park (200m).* ✦⑧

22

⑤ Turn L and stay on the track to the road (450m). Don't follow the track opposite but take the winding heath path R of it, up R of the war memorial on its hillock (250m), ★ Keep to the same path, round R, down to the lane (250m). Slightly R (20m) on the other side, take the path through the trees to the car park (100m). ✳

⑥ Immediately outside the vehicle exit, take the track to the cricket field (60m). Cross diagonally to the corner L of the pavilion (150m) and bear L on the heath path (150m).

⑦ Just after a side path back R, turn R down to the road (100m). Cross to the path opposite and go on, over the ridge tracks (200m) down the other side to the junction of bridleways outside the corner of the fields (200m). Follow the horse track down between the wood and field, past the houses R and the valley path L (200m),✦ up the sunken track (200m) and round the L bend past the cemetery (50m). Cross the cemetery drive and go up the path through the pines (100m).

⑧ Carry on up beside the track from the road past Barnett Hill, the house on the top, and down to the road in Wonersh (850m).

⑨ Cross, slightly R, to the green and follow the L hedge round to the road junction at the Pepper Pot and *Grantley Arms* (350m). Turn R along The Street (200m).

⑩ On the R curve, L of the road, go through the covered gateway (see high frieze) and the memorial garden to the church. Return to the road via the church drive (200m). Carry on (L) along the pavement and out of the village (200m).

⑪ At the bend take Chinthurst Lane R up the hillside. The Bramley Wey is visible below L (350m).

⑫ Between houses on top, bear R up Chinthurst Hill drive (300m).

⑬ Cut across the U-bend to the track and take the steepest path up to the tower on top (200m). ↘

With your back to the tower door the great distant eminence almost ahead (SE) is the Leith Hill range. Below, the houses slightly L, are part of Wonersh and above them is Barnett Hill with the eponymous Red Cross house in the trees. Beyond it L, the Blackheath pines are visible further round the ridge. The South Downs are far R.

When you descend, St Martha's Hill is ahead with the North Downs behind it. Flashing windscreens of A25 traffic may be seen climbing to Newlands Corner ½R. Guildford Cathedral is visible beyond the Hogs Back through the notch in the chalk ridge with the River Wey. Beyond the cathedral are Bagshot Heath and Swinley Forest on the Tertiary Sands eminence in front of Bracknell. The telecommunications mast (325°) is 21 km/13 miles away at Old Dean, overlooking Camberley.

⑭ The doorway faces SE. Walk northwards over the hill. Descend towards the L edge of the distant St Martha's Hill then keep to downhill paths (250m), through the boundary to the car park (250m).

Great Tangley Manor House

12 Blackheath and Albury

About 8.7 km/5½ miles on the Lower Greensand; hilly heath, woodland and pasture. The Blackheath paths are confusing. Shady in summer; good in winter. OS maps 1:25000 145 Guildford, 1:50000 186 Guildford +187 Dorking.

Start from Blackheath village car park, TQ 036 462.

Linking walks   11★   **The Drummond Arms** ☎ 01483 202039
㉖❋ ㉗✚ ㉘❋ ㉚✡ ㉜❋   **The Percy Arms** ☎ 01483 561765

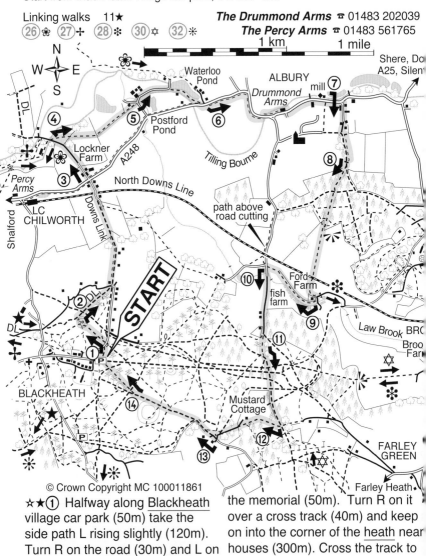

© Crown Copyright MC 100011861

★★① Halfway along <u>Blackheath</u> village car park (50m) take the side path L rising slightly (120m). Turn R on the road (30m) and L on the first side path. Avoid the R fork and soon ascend onto the hillock L of the memorial (200m).

② Cross the top of the hillock to the bridleway on the other side of the memorial (50m). Turn R on it over a cross track (40m) and keep on into the corner of the <u>heath</u> near houses (300m). Cross the track to the path beside the garden and carry on down the hillside then on tarmac over the railway bridge to the A248 (800m). (**Percy Arms** and Chilworth Station 500m L)

③ Cross and walk down the drive past Lockner Farm (400m). ❀

④ Just before the bridge (mill leat) turn back R through the fields (site of the Admiralty gunpowder works), past a pond far L and beside a garden to <u>Postford</u> Pond (650m).

⑤ Follow the lane over the bridge L, past offices (which replaced Postford Mill) and on (250m). At the bend take the path R between Waterloo Pond and Tilling Bourne to the road, A248 (250m). Turn L.

⑥ Follow the pavements L all the way to the **Drummond Arms L** in <u>Albury</u> (700m). Carry on through the village past the mill L (300m) and the trout pond L (150m).

⑦ Where the road bends L, turn R into the estate yard. If the office is open ask to see the pigeon house. Follow the drive to the top and go on up the path to the track in the trees (200m). Keep on ahead up the sunken track (200m

⑧ At the beginning of the wood, just after the cross track linking the fields, bear R out of the sunken track over the hilltop (200m). Cross the track and carry on down to the edge of the pines (300m). In the field go L along the fence past the corner of the wood and straight down to the railway (300m). Cross the rails to the sunken path in the trees (50m). Follow it round L of <u>Ford Farm</u> (150m). ✳

⑨ At the drive turn R (10m) and R again into the field. Pass R of the fish ponds and carry on beside the <u>lynchet</u> to the lane (450m).

⑩ Turn L over Law Brook. Keep on up the sandy lane to the top house (500m). ✿ At the fork go straight up the middle path (200m).

⑪ Over the brow, bear L on the cross track which curves R over several level forest tracks (200m). Stay ahead to the next brow (150m) and down to the crossing public footpath (100m).

⑫ Turn back R up the slope past Mustard Cottage R (250m) and continue on the sandy drive past other tracks joining R, round down L to the drive junction (250m).

⑬ Turn R. Follow the boundary track until it bends L (200m) ✳ and continue on the straight track through the heath, over a rise (300m) to the cross track just before the next rise (200m).

⑭ Fork R to the car park (200m).

Boletus has many species which are found in heaths and pinewoods. Some are edible; some are poisonous. They are easily recognised: usually brown with stout stalks and deep caps but no gills. The spores are produced in tubes which open as pores on the underside. *Boletus edulis* is called *bun mushroom* because it looks like a bun and *porcini* from the italian. In some countries it is harvested commercially in the wild. The toadstool is an ephemeral fruiting body for spore production. The permanent fungal body is a mass of hyphæ (threads) spread like a mould through the soil. The hyphæ invade conifer and birch roots for mutual benefit, in the symbiotic partnership, *mycorrhiza*. Fungi have chromosomes like plants and animals but are now considered a kingdom, with the moulds and yeasts.

13 Elstead, Cutt Mill and Puttenham Common

About 9.3 km/5¾ miles with a short cut of 1.3 km/¾ mile. Lower Greensand, River Wey, farmland, bluebell woods and confusing heath; fairly shady; soft sand in summer. OS maps 1:25000 145 Guildford, 1:50000 186 Aldershot.

Start from the Elstead long lay-by near the church, SU 905 435; or from a Puttenham Common car park, Middle, SU 912 458 or Top, SU 920 461.

Linking walks 1✦ 6✾ 14✪
21★ 22✪ 23✡ 27✿

Woolpack 01252 703106
Elstead Mill 01252 703333
Golden Fleece 702349
Little Barn Cafe 705023

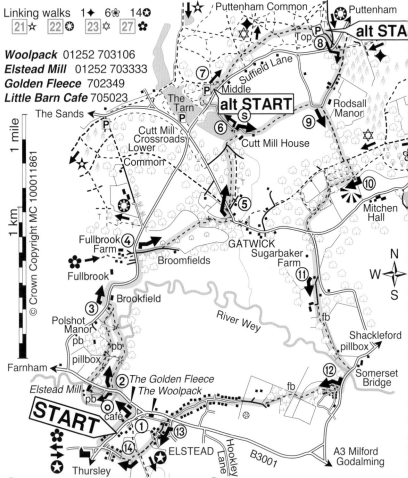

① From the Elstead lay-by go R on the pavement to the village green (300m). (**Woolpack** 100m R). Bear L past the shops (see WWII rifle loop holes in the Bargate wall on the main road) then L down the B3001 over the River Wey (300m).

② Either go R along the river bank path to the next road (600m) or

⊙ Continue to the drive L (40m) and follow it to **Elstead Mill** (150m). Turn R along the wall of the mill and cross the B3001 to the verge (60m). Go L to the next field (20m) and cross it, diverging slightly from the R edge, to the pillbox in the tall trees at the corner of a garden (200m). Carry on ahead along the

26

garden fence (100m) then ½L over the next field and through the trees (150m). In the next field turn R along the hedge (100m). After the house join the road L (40m).

③ Go R up the road winding R & L to Fulbrook Farm (500m). ✪☆

④ Opposite the Fulbrook track, turn R on the track to the gate L (halfway to Bloomfields) (200m). In the field diverge L from the track (300m) and go on through trees to the road at Gatwick (250m).

⑤ Turn L (40m). Immediately after the track, take the bridleway R and fork L on the path through Lower Puttenham Common (400m). Cross the track at the bend to Cutt Mill Pond and go R, along the dam, round the corner to the building (120m) and onto the tarmac drive.

Ⓢ *Short cut of 1.3 km/¾ mile: Turn R along the winding drive to the cottage (150m) and continue on the path to the lane (400m). Turn R to the next bend (100m).*➜⑨

⑥ *Follow the drive L to the road (250m). ☆ Go into the trees opposite and take the R rising path (40m) then turn R to the car park. Cross to the gateway (150m). ✿✦*

⑦ *From the vehicle exit of Middle Car Park take the path NE near the road, soon diverging from it, to the adjacent side paths R & L. Just after this (20m), branch R. Keep on to the steep slope ahead after a cross path (400m). Ascend (100m).*

⑧ *From Puttenham Common Top car park go out to the road (100m). Cross to the house and skirt R of the garden into the sunken track (100m). Go R to the tarmac and ahead past Rodsall Manor House (300m) to the first bend (50m).*

⑨ Go down the side path and up to the T-junction in the wood (400m).✿ Turn L (25m) & R (120m).

⑩ Turn R on the crosspath just before the field. Stay near the edge of the wood (200m) and slighly L into the fenced section with conifers L and paddocks R (150m). At the end of the conifers turn into the field (10m) and go round the R edge down to the road junction (200m). Walk along Attleford Lane, opposite, past Sugarbaker Farm R to the first roadside house R (300m).

⑪ Bear R on the farm track. After the buildings keep on ahead into the wood, over the footbridge, past a pillbox and across the riverside field to Somerset Bridge (550m). Cross. Walk up the road (150m)

⑫ Turn R on the curving side road (60m). After the 2nd house, take the path R up to the field and make for the top R corner (250m). Turn R on the path, soon in trees (300m). Join the lane and stay ahead between the houses on Ham Lane to the B3001 in Elstead (700m).

⑬ Cross into Springfield opposite (30m). Turn R along Back Lane past one house (40m) then L up the hill to the staggered cross path on top (400m). ✪

⑭ Avoid the path L. Go down outside (L of) the field and on to the crossroads at Elstead Church

Nettle stings are trichomes - plant hairs. Their cellulose walls are hardened at the tips by silica, SiO_2. These prick and break releasing several chemicals. Formic acid is the irritant. Acetyl choline is the main neurotransmitter in animals; perhaps amplifying the sting.

x25

14 The Moat, the Lion's Mouth and Elstead

About 8.8 km/5½ miles with an extension of 500m/¹⁄₃ mile in Elstead. Confusing heath, little shade; several short steep ascents; soft sand in summer, boggy bits in very wet seasons. OS maps 1:25000 145 Guildford 1:50000 186 Aldershot.

Start at The Moat car park, SU 899 416, or at Elstead, SU 905 435, from the long lay-by between the village green and the church on the Thursley road.

The Woolpack ☎ 01252 703106   Linking 13❁ 15✹ 16❖ [27]✿ [28]✦ [30]❊
The Golden Fleece ☎ 01252 702349
Elstead Mill ☎ 01252 703333
Little Barn Café ☎ 01252 705023

① From the Moat car park cross the road and take the track (400m).
② At the lane turn R. Watch out for the end of the L fence (100m). Just after it (30m), take the unofficial path L over the mound and ditch in the trees. Follow it, soon parallel with a fence L, to the open heath of Hankley Common (200m).

③ Go L on the major track (250m).
④ Take the next side-track R up to the T-junction (200m). Go L (150m) then diverge R on the track curving up through the trees ✦ Keep on up to the Lion's Mouth, a cleft where tracks cut through Riverbed Ridge (400m). (The Atlantic Wall is 100m beyond the cleft, on the L fork.)

5) Ascend R to the gravel top and go north along the ridge, towards the far telecommunications tower at Crooksbury Hill, then down a bit and up over Yagden Hill (1100m).✿

6) From the brow descend the N path (80m) and turn R down the track crossing the foot. When it curves R (200m) stay ahead, under the power cables (200m). Ignore tracks L & R and continue to the 5-way junction under trees (900m).

7) Don't make for Hankley Farm but turn R on the main track (400m). Continue on the lane across the brook (from Devils Punch Bowl) (500m) to Elstead Church (400m).

e) *Extension of 600m/⅓ mile to the village green and pubs: Turn L on the pavement to the village green (400m)* ⬤ *and pass R of the Woolpack on Back Lane (150m).*

f) *Turn R on the track between the houses just before the next road. Stay ahead on tarmac and track up to the 4-way path junction on top (300m). Turn L.*➧9)

8) Cross the road and walk up West Hill (150m) then up the path beside the field to the 4-way junction on top (100m). Turn R.

9) Go along the R edge of the fields (900m), L round the corner (40m) and R towards the wood on Ockley Common (200m). ✱✦

10) Just before the gate, take the track R under trees to the vehicle track (250m). Cross and continue ahead on the horse track over the heath to Pudmore Pond L (500m).

11) Just before the pond are two side paths L, 25m apart. Take the 2nd, with pines, on a boardwalk (on the ancient boundary mound of Thursley Common) and round the R bend at Thor's Stone which is camouflaged by lichens and mosses (200m). ✱ Go straight on over Thursley Bog along the boardwalk on the boundary mound (600m). Cross the path with the electricity poles to a T-junction (100m) and go R, round the Moat pond to the car park (150m).

Thursley Common has the richest dragonfly and damsel-fly fauna in Britain. The two groups make up the insect order Odonata. Juveniles are wingless and aquatic, preying on underwater insects and crustaceans.

These are the hawks of the insect world, catching other insects on the wing with forward mounted legs. Sight and computational skill enable them to vector in on fast-moving prey

Slender form distinguishes damsel-flies, though they may be longer than small dragonflies. The classification is based on wing-form. Dragonflies have different front and hind wings, spread when perched. Damsel-flies have similar wings, pressed together at rest. *Dragonflies of Great Britain & Ireland* Cyril O Hammond Harley 1996 116pp

15 Thursley Common and Village

About 8.5 km/5¼ miles. Confusing heath and ponds, soft sand in summer; good for birds, dragonflies and reptiles; best when the heather is in flower in August. OS maps 1:25000 145 Guildford + 133 Haslemere, 1:50000 186 Aldershot.

Start from the Moat (pond) car park, SU 899 416, or Thursley recreation ground, SU 899 398, or the lay-by in Old Portsmouth Road near the A3, SU 907 396.

14❉ 16✦ 18✿ 19❉ 30★ 32❀

Three Horseshoes
☎ 01252 703900

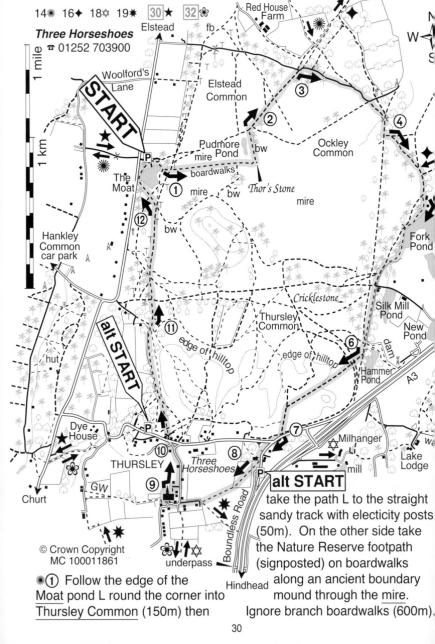

© Crown Copyright
MC 100011861

❉① Follow the edge of the Moat pond L round the corner into Thursley Common (150m) then

take the path L to the straight sandy track with electicity posts (50m). On the other side take the Nature Reserve footpath (signposted) on boardwalks along an ancient boundary mound through the mire. Ignore branch boardwalks (600m).

After Pudmore Pond L, go round the L bend at Thor's Stone (covered by mosses) to the track (200m).

② Turn R on this <u>heath</u> track to the vehicle track (<u>500m</u>). ✦

③ Go R on this winding track to the L bend (600m). Don't turn but stay ahead to the stream (150m).

④ After the bridge (100m), take the side track L (50m) and fork R past the converging path L (250m) and the fenced side-track L (60m). Stay ahead (150m).

⑤ At the shed L, bear L on the side path to Fork Pond (100m). Continue at the edge to the very end of the pond (300m) then curve R to re-join the main path (150m). Carry on along the fence (200m). Pass the exit track and house L and join the major track where the boundary bends L (400m). Keep on to the side path rising ½R (100m)✿

⑥ Go up this side path, across two curving paths (100m), over the brow (250m) ↘↗ and across the flat top (250m). This was the London to Portsmouth Road! Bear L on the wider track to the edge of Thursley Common (150m).

Cross the boundary track and go out to the road (20m).

⑦ Turn R (50m) then fork L down the Old Portsmouth Road (200m).

⑧ Opposite the houses L (former *Red Lion*), after the buildings, take the oblique path across the field to the corner (250m) and up the next field to the house (250m). ✳ Walk down the drive to the bend in the road (150m) and ahead up to <u>Thursley Church</u> (100m). ★❀

⑨ Go round the church and leave by the back gate (N) (100m). Turn L along the road and fork L beside <u>Street House</u> to the end (300m). The ***Three Horseshoes*** is 150m R.

⑩ Cross the road into the track between houses. When it bends R (30m), go down the side path ahead, with paths converging R & L, to the field (300m). Carry on beside the field (500m).

⑪ When the path bends L, at the end of the field, branch off on the path ahead over the wide sandy track (200m) to the oblique cross path from the boardwalk R (500m).

⑫ Bear L. Follow the path L of the pond round to the car park (300m).

Mire is the collective name for marsh, swamp, bog, fen - waterlogged terrain. Waterlogging excludes air and anæ-robic decay of vegetation makes peat. Peat acid pickles bodies, hence the Iron Age mire men found in recent years. Ombrotrophic (cloud fed) bog is raised on surfaces where high rainfall promotes *sphagnum* moss that holds water. Geotrophic mires form when rivers and shallow lakes silt up and vegetation collects dust. Ancient peat has evidence for palæoclimatologists: pollen grains from ancient vegetation and tree rings in logs. Northern mires have volcanic dust from Iceland which mark layers in peat which allow dating and correlation eg Hekla 3, *c*.1000BC.

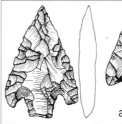

actual size

Flint arrow heads found on the slopes of Thursley Common by local people. They are Neolithic style but working in flint persisted well into the Bronze Age. Herodotus says the Ethiopians in Xerxes' army used stone-tipped arrows during the invasion of Greece, 480 BC. Drawings by Audrey Graham

16 Rodborough, Ockley and Royal Commons

About 7.2 km/4½ miles with an extension of 1.0 km/²⁄₃ mile. Confusing heath and woodland, half shady. Impassable in ⑩ in wet seasons. OS maps 1:25000 145 Guildford 1:50000 186 Aldershot.

Start at Rodborough Common (pay) car park, SU 937 418, reached from the A3 access road southwards from Milford or in Hookley Lane, Milford, SU 914 439.

Linking walks 14❖ 15✦ 17✹

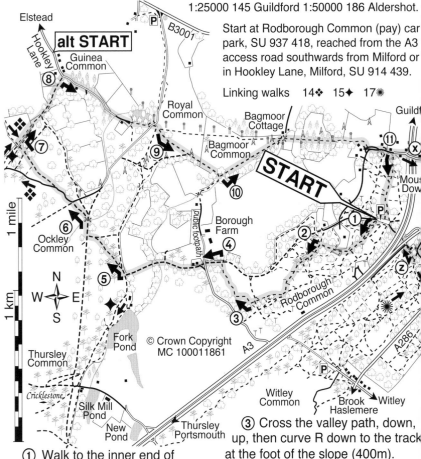

© Crown Copyright MC 100011861

① Walk to the inner end of Rodborough Common car park and take the side path L, forking R or L, level at first (200m) then down to the 5-way junction in trees opposite a house 100m far R (100m). Bear R down past the garden fence and lumpy ground to a cross path near the bottom of the dry valley (200m).

② Turn L. Pass lots of side paths and join the L converging path on a rise to trees (400m). Soon after it (30m) diverge R on the path, down, up, outside the trees (100m).

③ Cross the valley path, down, up, then curve R down to the track at the foot of the slope (400m).

④ Turn L (100m) and cross the Borough Farm drive. Slightly L, go on past the houses and eventually between fields to the boundary track at Ockley Common (600m). ✦

⑤ Turn R (70m) and fork L to the converging path R (300m). Keep on to the broad sandy path (50m).

⑥ Go R (100m). Cross the stream and fork L to the hard track (150m). Stay ahead (150m) ❖ then fork R on a lesser track into trees. Keep on to the corner of the field (400m).

32

⑦ Turn R either along the edge of the field or on the path outside the hedge. These two paths join after the field (150m). Carry on down (80m) and join the broader track, from R, to Hookley Lane with its row of houses (300m). Turn R.

⑧ Continue on the road through Guinea Common (450m) and on the drive through the garden at the end (100m). Go on through the trees (L path of 2) to the end of the pond on Royal Common (200m).

⑨ Cross the drive to the path junction (30m R of power cables) (30m). Take the public footpath (ie between the path parallel with the electricity posts and the path diverging from the drive) (550m).

⑩ At the T-junction turn L through Bagmoor Common, eventually crossing the footbridge, 50m R of Bagmore Cottage (500m). Stay ahead over the fields (100m), between tree plantations (250m) and along the track between fields to house drives (200m). Go up the L slope (30m) and L on the unmade road to the first house R (200m).

ⓧ *Extension of 1.0 km/²⁄₃ mile via Mousehill Manor: Continue on the winding road over the A3 bridge to the high garden wall L in the trees (350m) then turn R on Mousehill Manor drive. Pass the house and go on along the drive of the next house to the road (300m).*

ⓨ *Turn R on the pavement. Cross where convenient before the curve (200m) and diverge L on the unmade road with houses (250m).*

ⓩ *At the L bend stay ahead into the common (50m). Turn R on the first side path, past the pump house to the road (100m). Cross to the path opposite and follow it to the tunnel under the A3 (30m). Go through to the car park (150m).*

⑪ Before this house 30m, turn R up the path to the top of Mousehill Down (150m). Continue ahead down to the car park (300m). ✳

Common land is generally open to the public for air and exercise but is not the property of the public or the nation. It is remnants of land called *waste* in early documents which was not ploughed for crops but used for grazing, building materials, firewood, peat cutting, etc. As the population expanded, the waste was shared out between communities who marked their portions with mounds or hedges. It now belonged to the lord of the manor and commoners; they could use it for themselves but not work it for private profit or sell it. Fences were not permitted to divide or enclose it.

Encouraging enterprise, there was the tendency in the Middle Ages to parcel shared arable land into private farms. Much of the waste was taken up in the process. Later on, the Enclosure Acts were used to overcome recalcitrant commoners. In general, only the least useful commons and village greens survived. Surrey has large commons because of heath on the Greensand and Tertiary Sands, and waterlogging on the London Clay.

In the 20th century commoners lost sight of their commons. Employment was moving away from the land. A commoner might have the rights to graze two cows but was not allowed to erect a fence or was not prepared to share the herding. Coal replaced firewood and peat. Lords of manors became the only visible owners and were able to sell. Commons were bought by the Forestry Commission, the army, boroughs, builders and preservation societies. There are still a few registered commoners.

The Common Lands of England and Wales
W G Hoskins & L Dudley Stamp 1963 Collins

17 Witley Common and Mare Hill

About 7.7 km/4¾ miles with an extension of 2.1 km/1¼ miles. Confusing heath; best when the heather is in flower (August); half shady, gentle slopes. OS maps 1:25000 145 Guildford, 1:50000 186 Aldershot.

Pay at Webb Road car park, SU 933 409. There are free car parks on the route: Lea Coach Road, SU 927 398, next to the cemetery at Milford Common, SU 941 413, and Roke Lane on Mare Hill, SU 937 399. Rodborough Common car park is on the extension, SU 937 418.

Linking walks 16✿ 18✵ 24✴

The Star
☎ 01428 684656
The White Hart
☎ 01428 683695

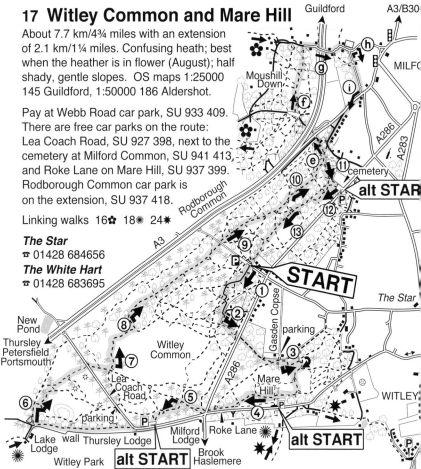

① At the cross track E of Webb Road car park, go up through the pine wood. Keep to the hard path round several L and R bends to the NT Witley Centre buildings (450m).
② Turn R on the path past the end of the building with boundary mound R (70m). At the end of the mound, turn L on the lesser path R of a mound then diverge to the A286 opposite a track (150m). Cross and go up Mare Hill to the corner of a garden (200m). Keep on (50m) and bear L on the next track, outside the garden fence in the trees, past the end of the road with houses (50m).

③ After the road (50m) branch up up R (30m) then curve L. Go over the rise (60m) and R on the side path (20m). Curve R & L up the steep path on to the ridge (200m). Turn R to the summit (150m). ✴✵
④ Stay on the ridge path down to the road junction (500m). Cross the A286 into the trees (40m) and fork L to the first cross path (150m).
⑤ Go L, round R & L bends, to the car park (300m) then along the road to the bend at the gatehouse of Witley Park (120m). Stay ahead on the path outside the wall to the bend in the unmade road (700m).

34

⑥ Just before this bend turn R on the path R of the wall (150m). Take the first side path R up to the track round the hillock (50m)(Amphibian & Reptile Conservation Trust). Go L round the slope (150m), back L on the side path (70m) and R on the parallel path (150m). When it bends R take the side path ahead across flat heath to the road in the trees (150m). Opposite, diverge on the path to the cross path (200m).

⑦ Turn L (200m). The path bends R to a T-junction (150m).

⑧ Turn L. Follow the path round a R bend (100m) then stay ahead, almost in a straight line to Webb Road (disused part) (800m).

⑨ There are two paths opposite. Take the L one. Watch out for the junction with a converging path R (350m). Stay ahead past another converging path R (80m) to the fork at the start of a L curve (150m).

⑩ Fork R. Stay ahead down past a cross path (250m) and over a rise to the side path back R, 20m from the large sand pit R (100m).

ⓔ *Extension of 2.1 km/1¼ miles to Moushill Down: Stay ahead (70m). Watch out for a building L and bear L on the path past it to the road (100m). Cross. Follow the path opposite to the tunnel under the A3 (30m). Go through to Rodborough Common car park (100m).* ✿

ⓕ *Near the middle of the car park take the side path R into the trees, up to the top of Mousehill Down (450m) and down the other side to the houses (150m).*

ⓖ *Go R over the A3 to the high garden wall L in the trees (350m).*

ⓗ *Turn R along the Moushill Manor drive. Go past the house*

and on on along the drive of the next house to the road (300m).

ⓘ *Turn R and cross where convenient before the curve (200m). Diverge L on the unmade road past houses (250m). At the L bend take the path ahead up through trees (150m) and fork L near the sandpit.*

⑪ Stay on this path, avoiding all side paths R (100m), to the Milford Common car park (100m).

⑫ Leave the car park by the path which is not beside the cemetery (60m). Turn L on the first cross path Follow it round a R bend (100m) to a 3-way junction (50m) and go up L through the trees (150m).

⑬ Just after the trees fork L. Stay ahead to Webb Road near the car park (500m).

Heathers are in the ERICACEAE, the same family as rhododendrons and billberries. The three most common British heathers live on local heaths. Old plants have leaning stems up to 100cm; young plants flower at 10cm.

Calluna vulgaris, heather, ling: separate petals, pale mauve; overlapping moss-like leaves.

Erica cinerea, bell heather: petals form a tube, bright bluish purple; slender leaves in 3s, usually hairless.

Erica tetralix, cross-leaved heather mauve flowers like little balloons; leaves in 4s, hairy.

x2

R. ponticum is the most abundant Rhododendron in Britain. It is invasive and makes dense thickets on acid upland soils. Pollen shows it was indigenous before the last glaciation. It was reintroduced in the 16th century. Ornamentals grafted on R *ponticum* root-stocks revert when neglected.

18 Brook, Witley Park and Thursley

About 8.2 km/5 miles, with an extension of 4.3 km/2²/₃ miles to Thursley. Heath, pasture and woodland; short steep ascents. The heaths are confusing.
OS maps 1:25000 145 Guildford +133 Haslemere, 1:50000 186 Aldershot.

Start from Brook, parking in the side road opposite the pub, SU 930 380.
On the extension, Thursley car park is close to the route, SU 900 398.

Linking walks   15✿   17✳   19✳   20★   24★   26✩   30❖   32❀

The Dog & Pheasant 01428 682763
The Three Horseshoes 01252 703900

① At Brook enter the cricket field opposite the **Dog & Pheasant**. Go round the wall L and on through the wood to a tarmac drive (350m).

② Now follow the Greensand Way. Cross the A286 and walk along the side road beside the wall (400m). At Pine Lodge, the first house R, go through the wall, up the hill and between fields to the track (250m).

③ Turn R down the track. Stay ahead into the valley (300m), up through the wall (150m), over the drive of the next house, through the small fields (200m), over the drive of Heath Hall and up into the field.

④ Go R, along the edge, round a corner (200m) and through the hedge. Turn L to the road (150m).

ⓔ *Extension of 4¼ km/2¾ miles: Cross the road into the next field. Go straight over (120m), ½R down the slope (100m), ✳ R on the path at the foot, across the valley and up the Cosford Farm drive (200m).*

ⓕ *At the R bend, bear L down the track to a 4-way junction (500m). ★ Continue ahead on the farm drive (120m). Just before the house turn R up the diverging track (80m). At the fields take the oblique uphill branch track to a junction (100m) and continue to the top field (20m). Keep on obliquely to the hilltop then beside the A3 (150m).*

ⓖ *Pass under the A3 (70m) ✳ and over the lane into the field (30m). ✳ Cross the field obliquely to the gate in the trees 50m R of the lowest corner (350m). Go through the next field parallel with the L edge (250m) and on down the fields to Thursley (500m). ❖ Stay ahead on the road and fork R at Street House (400m). (**Three Horseshoes** 100m R) ✿*

ⓗ *Cross the road and follow the path between houses (200m). After the field turn R along the boundary of Thursley Common (400m). Pass round curves R & L (150m) and continue down beside the road to the exit at the road bridge (400m).*

Elstead
Churt

Thursley Common

alt START
Gw
Three Horseshoes
THURSLEY
P
A3
Gw
Boundless Road
Gw
underpass
Bedford Farm
ⓕ
ⓖ
underpass
dam
Hindhead

① *Cross the A3 (150m) and go R down the slip road (150m). Halfway down turn L on the tarmac drive then L down the farm track (250m). Stay ahead down the Millhanger drive, round the valley past Cosford Mill R (200m), up the path (150m) and ahead on the road (100m).* ➔⑥

Turn R (100m) and fork L to the A286 (80m) opposite the lodge of Witley Park. Continue over the A286 up Mare Hill on the main path parallel with Roke Lane to the summit (500m). Cross the path from the car park and go on to the next side path R (150m).

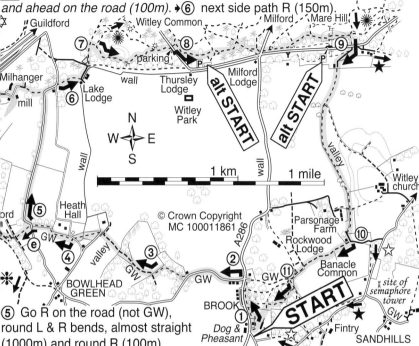

⑤ Go R on the road (not GW), round L & R bends, almost straight (1000m) and round R (100m).

⑥ When the road bends L at the farm drive, take the downhill path ahead (200m). Continue down the house drive into Witley Common (100m). At the L bend, take the side path R and turn L, past a wall L, to the first side path R (150m). ✳

⑦ Go R over the R flank of the hillock (Amphibian & Reptile CT) and down R of the Bronze Age barrow (500m) to Lea Coach Road (150m).

⑧ Continue on the path opposite (50m). Take the path R up round the top (300m), over a cross path (from the car park R) and round a L bend to the next cross path (200m).

⑨ Turn R to Roke Lane (80m). ★ Go down the drive opposite round a R bend (200m). Continue past the houses, over fields, up the valley to a cross path on top (1000m) and L of the farm house to the drive R of the next house (170m). Pass between the cottages (50m).☆

⑩ Turn R on the path between fields to Heath Hills Wood (500m).

⑪ Take the first side path L (GW) outside the field (60m) and turn R down through the wood until above the cricket field (250m). Turn down to it (30m) and cross the field to the road L of the house (150m).

19 Thursley, Emley Farm and Highfield Farm

About 9.3 km/5¾ miles. The extension of 2.2 km/1⅓ miles and short cut of 4.0 km/2½ miles can be used together. Hilly farm land on the Greensand with lots of stiles. OS maps 1:25000 133 Haslemere, 1:50000 186 Aldershot.

Start at Thursley Rec, SU 900 398, or Boundless Road car park, SU 898 378.

Linking walks 15✴ 18✳ 20✿ 22✿ 30◇ 32✳ 33✿   *The Three Horseshoes* ☎ 01252 703900

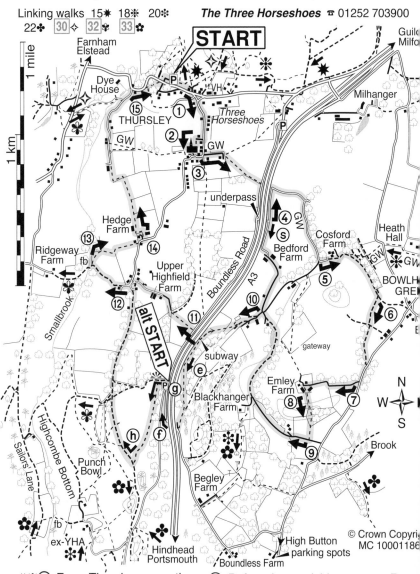

✴✳① From Thursley recreation ground walk into the village (100m) and turn R past Street House down The Street (300m).

② Before the roadside cottages R turn R on the track to the churchyard (100m). Go round Thursley Church anticlockwise to the road (100m).

③ Go down the road to the L bend (100m) and ahead up the drive to the field (150m).✳ Two RoWs cross obliquely. Take the path across the R corner and on along the R edge (400m). Turn R up Boundless Road beside the A3 (200m) and L through the underpass (50m).

⑤ *Short cut of 4 km/2½ miles: Turn R up the lane (250m). On top go round L & R bends and down the cart track past the farm to the 4-way junction (400m) then R.* ➔⑩

④ Walk down the lane L (200m), round the R bend and over the rise through the trees (650m).

⑤ Carry on round the L bend, past Cosford Farm (60m) and down over the stream (100m). Disregard a rising GW branch path in the trees and keep on outside fields at the foot of the hillside (350m).

⑥ Soon after the end of the wood turn R up the farm track between fields (200m). Continue over the cross track up to the road (200m). Walk up the road (R) (100m).

⑦ Turn R on the next drive. Keep on to Emley Farm (400m).

⑧ Opposite the house R take the footpath L beside the 2nd barn, up over the hilltop and down through the trees (200m). Continue down the field to the farm drive (100m). ✤

⑨ Turn R past houses R (150m). When the drive bends down L to Blackhanger Farm (350m) ✳✿ stay ahead down the track into the trees, round past the pond L, over the causeway dam (550m) and up to a 4-way junction (150m). Turn L.

⑩ Follow the track into the farm (120m). Opposite the house drive, bear R up the side track. Keep on ever upwards to the top field

(200m). Continue to the hilltop obliquely (L) then L near the A3 to the walkers' subway (200m).

ⓔ *Extension of 2¼ km/1⅓ miles: Stay ahead L of the A3 and down to the minor road (650m).*

ⓕ *Go under the A3, up the road.*

ⓖ *At the N end of the car park, after the junction (50m), turn L up the track beside the field (60m) and take the first side path L up through* Hindhead Common *to the major heath track on the edge of the* Devils Punch Bowl *(600m).* ✿

ⓗ *Go R down the track past the cross track (450m) and ahead to the tarmac lane (800m). Turn L.* ➔⑫

⑪ Go under the A3 (70m). Turn R between the roads (40m) and L into the field. Aim straight over for the gap in the trees in the dip (300m) and walk up the track R (100m). Continue on the farm drive to the road (250m). Turn L (25m) then R.

⑫ Go down the steepening side lane (60m). When it bends L to the houses continue ahead down the steep track to the bottom (250m). ✤

⑬ Don't cross Smallbrook but ascend R to the fields above the stream and follow the winding path outside fields to the road (350m).

⑭ Go L on the road briefly (30m) then take the footpath L from the drive of Hedge Farm. Go round outside the garden (100m) and R, down between the fields, with L & R bends, to the lane (600m). ✧ Keep on ahead down to the road (600m).

⑮ Follow the road R until it bends L uphill out of the valley (100m). Diverge R up the steep footpath ahead to the road (200m). Cross into Thursley recreation ground.

20 Gibbet Hill, Punch Bowl & Blackhanger Farm

About 8.7 km/5½ miles with an extension of 1.1 km/²/₃ miles.
Heath, pasture, woodland; short steep slopes, grand views.
OS 1:25000 133 Haslemere,1:50000186 Aldershot.

Start: Devils Punch Bowl car park (NT pay), Hindhead, SU 890 357.

Linking 18★ 19✳ 21◉ 22☆
30◇ 32★ 33◆ 34♣ 44✪ 45✧

Devils Punch Bowl Hotel
☎ 01428 606565
Devils Punch Bowl Café
☎ 01428 608771

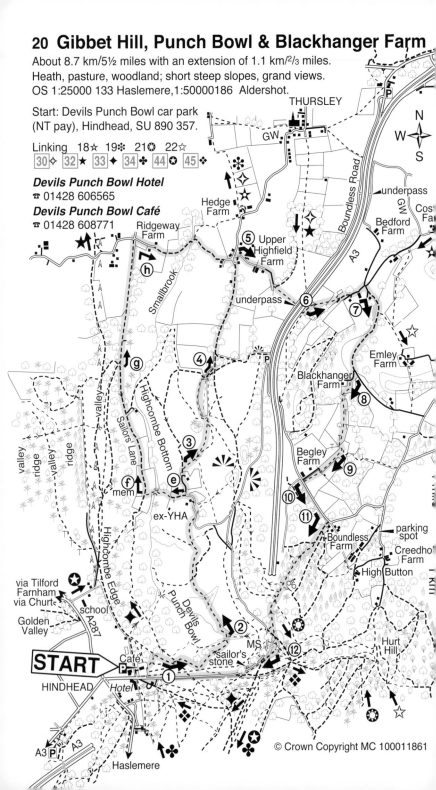

© Crown Copyright MC 100011861

① Cross the Hindhead car park from the ***café*** to the view point on the rim of the Devils Punch Bowl (100m). ⤵ Turn R on the path below it (120m) and L down the side path. Avoid a steep side path back L (30m) and carry on round the L curve (150m) down to the spring in the narrow valley (350m).

② Disregarding side turns, stay on the same path, undulating around the side of the combe to the tarmac lane at the end (800m). Go down the lane L, past houses and round the L curve to the R bend (200m).

ⓔ *Extension of 1.1 km⅔ mile: Turn L from the lane, down the track past the gardens to the brook (200m) and up to Sailors' Lane, a track between fields (100m). Turn R. Pass a cottage down R (550m) and go up the flank of the combe to the 4-way junction on the L bend at the top (350m). ★✧*

ⓖ *Turn R on the bridleway along the ridge, soon sinking into a deep stony cleft between fields (800m).*

ⓗ *At the lane turn R up past the houses. Continue down the rocky track (450m), over the Smallbrook footbridge ❄☆ and up the track and lane from houses to the junction (300m). Turn L (25m) then R. ➤⑤*

③ Descend past Gnome Cottage (150m). After the cattle grid bear R up the side of the combe to a field on top (450m). Go through or L of the field to the bottom gate (250m).

④ Turn R (100m) and fork L then bear L downhill. Keep on under trees outside fields to the lane junction (700m) and the drive of Upper Highfield Farm R (25m).

⑤ Walk up the drive. Continue to the end of the tarmac (250m) and down the farm track (120m). Enter the L field at the end. Take the bisecting line up from the corner and over towards the A3 (300m).

⑥ Cross the little road and turn R to the subway (50m). Go under the A3 and turn L on the path which curves R and descends obliquely to the exit near the middle of the bottom edge of the field (150m). Carry on down through the trees to the farm house (150m) and walk out along the drive L (100m).

⑦ At the 4-way junction, turn R to the long pond (200m) ☆ and carry on up to Blackhanger Farm (500m).

⑧ Turn R down the drive (100m). Just before the garden enter the L field and skirt round the garden to the top corner (100m). Cross the belt of trees to the next field (40m) and go round the L edge (300m).

⑨ At the end, exit L to the path junction (40m) and turn R along the narrow field (200m). Cross the next field to the R corner (100m).

⑩ Join the lane at Begley Farm. Turn L to Boundless Farm (300m).

⑪ Next to the first house, turn R up the forest track to the R bend (170m). Keep on up past the public footpath with a staggered crossing (450m) ❀ and round a L curve (70m). Continue less steeply over an oblique sunken track (150m) to the trig point on the flat top of Gibbet Hill (100m). ⤵ ❖✪◆❖

⑫ Turn R on the level track (SW) to the tarmac drive (Old Portsmouth Road) at the opposite edge of the hill (120m). Go L down it, past the murdered sailor's stone R (read the back & front) (100m), to the NT car park in Hindhead (700m) or the ***Devils Punch Bowl Hotel*** 50m L.

21 Grayswood, Inval, Hurt Hill and Gibbet Hill

About 7.5 km/4²/₃ miles with an extension of 2.3 km/1½ miles to the Devils Punch Bowl in Hindhead. Tricky navigation and steep slopes, oak and pine wood, long views. OS maps 1:25000 133 Haslemere, 1:50000 186 Guildford.

Start from the roadside at the top end of Grayswood village green, SU 917 346. On the extenson start from Devils Punch Bowl car park (NT/pay), SU 890 357.

The Wheatsheaf ☎ 01428 644440   Linking 20❁ 22✿ 23◇ 33 ✳ 34 ✿ 45 ❁
Devils Punch Bowl Hotel ☎ 01428 606565
Devils Punch Bowl Café ☎ 01428 608771

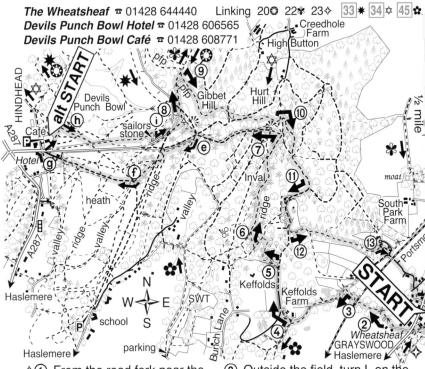

◇① From the road fork near the school at the top of Grayswood village green, turn R up the tarmac path beside the shop, to the A286 (250m) (50m L of the **Wheatsheaf**). Cross the road and go down the shared drive opposite (120m).

② Bear R down the path between the gardens into the valley (150m). After the stream continue in the same direction up through the trees to the railway (London-Portsmouth) (200m). Turn L (30m) to the steps to cross the rails and return on the other side (30m) then carry on up through the wood to a field (100m).

③ Outside the field, turn L on the undulating path (40m) and over the boardwalk up to the track with sides (50m). Cross the R mound to the fence and carry on, past the pond R below, up the sunken track. Pass the garden gate R and continue into the field below Keffold's Farm (200m). Keep on around the top edge into the trees and past the house R to the bridleway (150m). ✿

④ Turn back R a bit (10m) and go up the edge of the garden. Keep on to the tarmac drive (120m). Turn R up the hard track to the end of the fields L (300m).

⑤ Go L up the side path after the field (80m), round R & L bends to the track (100m) and up L (100m).

⑥ Take the next side path R which converges on the Inval ridge path. Keep on, down round a L bend (400m) to a very oblique cross path (120m). Turn R down the edge of the hill to the next junction (200m).

⑦ Turn L away from the edge past the Temple of the Four Winds (80m). Stay ahead, ultimately down to the complex junction in the cleft (550m). Either continue ahead to the trig point, up steep side paths L from the steep track (150m). or ✦ⓔ

ⓔ *Extension 2.3 km/1½ miles: Turn L briefly (10m) and go down the side path L (20m). After the gate turn R up beside the fence to the ridge path on top (250m).* ⬊ *Turn L (20m) and fork R (30m) then take the oblique side path R across the main ridge track (30m) down to the complex track junction (200m).*

ⓕ *Bear R on the track, curving L out of the trees. Continue ahead (South Downs visible L) to the road in Hindhead (700m) ⚬✳❂ near the* **Devils Punch Bowl Hotel** *L.*

ⓖ *Cross the National Trust car park R of the* **Devils Punch Bowl Café** *to the viewpoint overlooking the Devils Punch Bowl (150m).*

ⓗ *Turn R on the path along the brow, past a diverging side track down L (100m), to the cross path (100m). Bear L along the brow beside the "shelf" (position of the A3 until 2011): straight at first (350m) then curving L (100m).*

ⓘ *Climb the first steep side path R to the tarmac (old London-Portsmouth) road at the Sailor's Stone (60m). Go L up the tarmac*

(120m) and bear R across the flat top of Gibbet Hill to the trig point (100m). ⬊ ✦⑧

⑧ Start towards the Celtic cross (murdered sailor) memorial then fork along the R edge of the hill. Pass over the brow to the sunken track (80m). Cross it obliquely (40m R of the tarmac lane) ✽ and keep on down the steepening main path, curving R to where a public footpath branches R and L (200m). ❂

⑨ Turn R on the public footpath, round the hillside, winding and undulating, ultimately to a steep, deep-sunken track (500m). Cross it slightly R and carry on to the next major downhill path (150m). Cross that and carry on up to the next major path on a brow (250m).

⑩ Go through the gap to the out-of-sight parallel track then L down round a hairpin bend to a junction with paths R & L (300m). Stay on the main path round the side of the hill to a junction on a bend (250m).

⑪ Go round the R bend towards the house (200m). Pass the house and sheds and descend past the small fields L and a track R (250m).

⑫ At the end of the fields take the side track L, down round a R bend (150m). At the next R bend (50m) turn L off the main path, down through the trees eventually curving L to a garden (500m).

⑬ Turn R on the track past out-buildings to the house drive (80m). Walk under the railway (50m) down the unmade road with houses into the valley (250m). Cross the stream. Opposite the footbridge turn R up the steep footpath in the trees to the little road in Grayswood (80m). Go L to the main road (40m).

22 Grayswood, High Button and Witley Farm

About 8.5 km/5¼ miles with an extension of 1.5 km/1 mile and a short cut of 400m/¼ mile. Woodland on the Greensand and grassland on the Weald Clay. OS maps 1:25000 133 Haslemere, 1:50000 186 Guildford.

Start from the roadside at the top end of Grayswood village green, SU 917 346.

Linking walks 19✤ 20☆ 23✳ 33✤ 34✛ 45✳

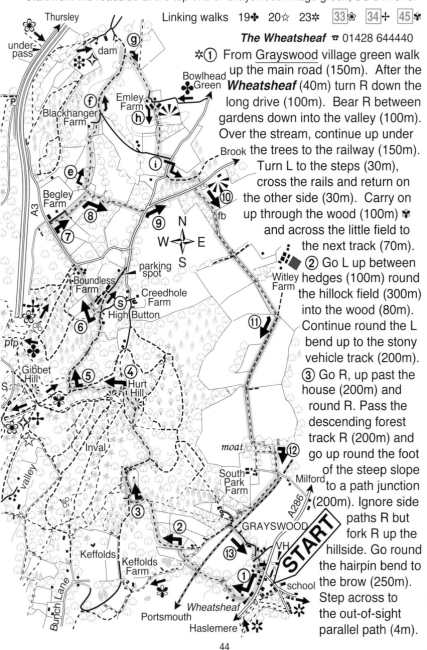

The Wheatsheaf ☎ 01428 644440

✳① From <u>Grayswood</u> village green walk up the main road (150m). After the *Wheatsheaf* (40m) turn R down the long drive (100m). Bear R between gardens down into the valley (100m). Over the stream, continue up under the trees to the railway (150m). Turn L to the steps (30m), cross the rails and return on the other side (30m). Carry on up through the wood (100m) ✤ and across the little field to the next track (70m).

② Go L up between hedges (100m) round the hillock field (300m) into the wood (80m). Continue round the L bend up to the stony vehicle track (200m).

③ Go R, up past the house (200m) and round R. Pass the descending forest track R (200m) and go up round the foot of the steep slope to a path junction (200m). Ignore side paths R but fork R up the hillside. Go round the hairpin bend to the brow (250m). Step across to the out-of-sight parallel path (4m).

④ Take the side path W away from the edge, initially down round the hill, then winding to a cross track (200m). Ascend L to a steep side track in a cleft (150m). ☆❀✢❖

⑤ Descend through forest and pass L of a house to the track junction at High Button (650m).

ⓢ *Short cut of 400m/¼ mile: Stay ahead to the road (350m). Bear L to the junction (100m) and continue over the rise (300m). ✦⑨*

⑥ Just before the track-fork, turn L on the side path in the trees (20m) and branch R towards the barns (60m). Go along the drive from the barnyard of Boundless Farm to the houses and out to the road (300m). Carry on along the road (L) (350m).

⑦ Turn R into the field beside the drive of Begley Farm. Diverge very slightly from the L edge and carry on along the R fence in the narrow field to the hedge bend L (350m).

ⓔ *Extension of 1.5 km/1 mile to Emley Farm: Turn into the adjacent field L (40m) and go round the R edge to the end (350m). Carry on through the trees to the next field (40m) and skirt round the bottom of the garden to the drive of Black-hanger Farm (100m). Go R up the drive to the R bend (100m).*

ⓕ *Turn L on the track down round the foot of the hill (400m).*

ⓖ *Halfway along the pond look out for the side path up R. Ascend through the trees, R of the hedge. Keep on to Emley Farm and between the buildings (400m).*

ⓗ *Take the path R between the barns, up the R edge of the field (150m), into the wood, straight down (100m) and across the field to the farm drive (100m).*

ⓘ *Turn L (100m), R down the road (100m) and L along the forest track (250m). Watch out for the side path R and follow it to the road (50m). Go R (40m) then L. ✦⑩*

⑧ Turn R on the winding path in the trees. Cross the stream and go on into the field (150m). Follow the R edge (100m) and go through the the end of the wood to the road (150m). Turn L (50m).

⑨ Bear R at the junction. Watch out for the access to the field at the end of the R wood (350m).

⑩ Go R down the edge of the fields to the end of the belt of trees R (350m). The escarpment far L is the Hascombe Hills. Carry on between fields, over the footbridge and farm track (200m) and ahead to a track from Witley Farm (500m).

⑪ Go R over the rise (450m) and on into the wood (400m). Just after access to the moat (40m), fork L on the unofficial path between the little ponds to the field (150m).

⑫ Turn R along the edge of the field to the farm drive (120m). Cross into the field opposite and go along the L edge near the railway (Portsmouth line) (300m). Continue down into the wooded valley, over the culvert and up to the track junction (150m).

⑬ Pass under the railway bridge (50m) and down the unmade road past houses into the valley (250m). Cross the stream. Opposite the end of the footbridge, ascend the steep footpath in the trees to the little road (80m). Turn L past the churchyard to the A286 and Grayswood village green (40m).

23 Grayswood and Frillinghurst

About 6.8 km/4¼ miles with an extension of 1.5 km/1 mile and a short cut of 2.4 km/1½ miles. Farmland and woodland on the Weald Clay, shady. Avoid in wet seasons. OS maps 1:25000 133 Haslemere 1:50000 178 Aldershot

Start from the roadside at the top end of Grayswood village green, SU 917 346.

Linking walks   21✧ 22✽ 27✽ 45❂

The Wheatsheaf ☎ 01428 644440

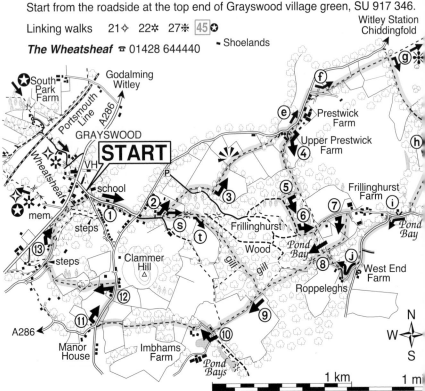

© Crown Copyright MC 100011861

✧✽❂① At the top of <u>Grayswood</u> village green, fork L on the road past the school to the T-junction (350m). Carry on down the track opposite, to the R bend (200m).

Ⓢ *Short cut of 2¼ km/1½ miles: Turn L (20m) then R of the small field into Frillinghurst Wood (150m).*

Ⓣ *After 2 horse bridges (50m), on the slight R curve, find the path R and diverge on it along the R edge of the wood (200m). Don't fork R. Descend gently (300m). Pass the side path R. Go on, into a <u>gill</u> (80m) and up the other side to the end of the wood (150m). Turn R. →⑨*

② Turn L on the footpath, L of fields, to the forest track from the road to Frillinghurst Wood (250m).

③ Cross into the field opposite and go R along the edge (200m). In the next field go L up the edge (200m). Stay ahead along the top of subsequent fields (300m) into the wood, after the house below, and down to a house drive at the road (150m). Go round the S-bend to the gateway of Upper Prestwick Farm (70m).

Ⓔ *Extension of 1½ km/1 mile: Stay on the road past the Prestwick Farm barns and cottages (350m).*

46

(f) *After the end cottage, take the drive R (80m). At the footpath enter the L field and cross obliquely to the corner of the hedge (40m). Stay ahead, L of the hedge (200m) then keep on over the fields, about 80m R of the road, to the row of trees on the rise (300m).* ✳

(g) *On the sunken path in the trees, turn R over the top of the hill and down. Continue on the vehicle track to the road at a pond (600m).*

(h) *Walk along the road R to the crossing path (60m) and enter the R field. Diverge from the road to the middle of the end hedge (200m). In the next field cross towards the trees at the far R corner (300m). Outside, drop to the road (30m).*

(i) *Walk down the road R (150m), round the L bend over the murky stream and up the slope (400m)*

(j) *Shortly before West End Barn, diverge R down the Roppelegh's drive (150m). Go round the U-bend at the house, up the other side and L across the hilltop into the wood (150m). Drop down the path to the stream and ascend to the field (150m). Turn L.* ➔(8)

(4) Turn into the gateway. Take the public footpath, just L of the house opposite. Go round the pond R and along the track outside the field, bearing R into the next field (150m). Go down the edge (100m) and on through the wood (200m).

(5) Turn R on the first side path (150m) and L on the track (250m).

(6) At the next junction follow the bridleway L (150m), out of the wood, past the farmhouse and down the Frillinghurst drive to the bottom end of the R field before the next houses (250m).

(7) Enter the field and cross obliquely to the gate near the bottom of the R fence (150m). Carry on along the bottom edge of the field to the end (200m).

(8) Exit at the corner. Stay ahead down into Frillinghurst Wood to the murky stream (100m) and up the other side beside the boundary mound (100m). Turn L just round a curve on top. Keep on until the adjacent field is visible L (300m).

(9) Continue to the next field (100m) and up the L hedge (250m). Before the house go through the gap to the adjacent field but continue in the same direction to the road opposite the Imbhams Farm pond (100m).

(10) Follow the road R (100m) round L & R bends (50m). After the farm drive, keep on R of fields (100m), through the wood over the hill, to the field (500m). Go round the R edge down to the road (200m).

(11) Follow the road R up to the cluster of three houses R (300m)

(12) Opposite the 2nd house take the path L past allotments into a field (120m). Carry on up the path converging on the top hedge (100m). In the next field pass the clump of trees making for the top, furthest corner (300m). ↘ Exit between gardens, down under a bridge to the track (100m). Descend to the lane via steps R or via the track L. Walk down the lane to the end of the tarmac (100m).

(13) Continue on the path down to the diverging descending side path R (70m). Go through the trees of Grayswood Common parallel with the A286 to the tarmac path (200m). Turn R for the village green (150m) or L for the *Wheatsheaf*. ✧✳✪

24 Witley, Enton and Sandhills

About 8.8 km/5½ miles with an extension of 1.1km/¾ mile around Banacle Common. Undulating farmland and wood; one short steep ascent; half shady; suitable for winter. OS maps 1:25000 133 Haslemere, 1:50000 186 Aldershot.

Start from Witley Lodge, SU 945 39, near Witley Church or the car park near Sweetwater Pond, SU 953 390. Witley Station (in Wormley), SU 948 379, has free parking at weekends.

Linking walks   17✹ 18★
25❀ 26♣ 28✳ 31✸ 32✿

The White Hart ☎ 01428 683695
The Star ☎ 01428 684656

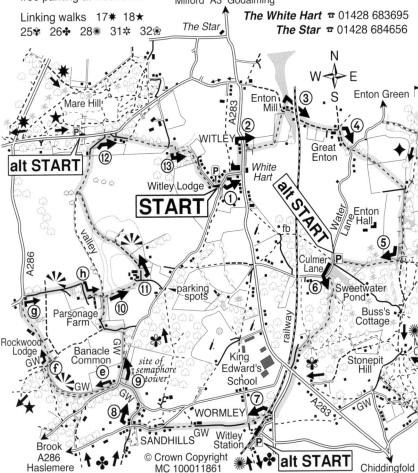

① From Witley Lodge go down the road past the church to the A283 opposite the *White Hart* (200m). Follow the pavement L and cross at the end of the high wall (150m).

② Take the footpath between the wall and house (50m) and ahead between fields (150m). Turn L into the long field and diverge from the L edge down towards the houses at the bottom corner (200m).

③ Outside turn R on the track, over Enton millstream, winding past the houses (100m), under the railway (Portsmouth line) and up to the T-junction of tracks (300m).

48

④ Turn R to the road (150m) ✳ and go up the path opposite to the field (150m). Keep on into the next field (70m) and over the brow down to the bottom corner near the house (250m). ❀ Cross the track and continue L of the field (Enton Hall up R), past the pond L (250m) to the gate (100m), and into the trees (40m). Fork R ahead to the track junction (60m). ✿❀

⑤ Turn R on the path in the trees (150m) and walk down beside the Enton Hall grounds. Cross the car park to the road (350m).

⑥ Go L on the road (100m). After Sweetwater Pond take the path L winding through the wood. Avoid a L fork (150m) and keep to the same path up L of a house (350m) and R of the next one to the track (100m). Turn L to the A283 (150m) (see King Edward's School R). Cross and carry on along Combe Lane opposite (300m). ❖

⑦ Round the L bend, after the first house R, take the footpath R over the railway and up beside the trees (200m). At the track junction, stay ahead to the house at the end of the track (400m) then on the footpath to the road at the hamlet of Sandhills (250m). Walk up the road L to the crossroads (250m)).

⑧ Turn R up Sebastopol Lane to the next road (150m) then L up to the T-junction on top (200m). ★

ⓔ *Extension of 1.1 km/¾ mile: Turn L (60m) and take the path R, GW, above the road. Follow the fence (Banacle Common) curving round R, avoiding side paths L, to the bridleway at the end (550m).*

ⓕ *Turn R to the fence corner (50m) and take the side path L*

eventually down to the road (450m). Stay ahead on the verge (40m).

ⓖ *Turn R on the drive (270m). At the fork continue ahead (150m).*

ⓗ *Round the bend R (100m) take the path L beside Parsonage Farm to the cross path (100m).* ➜⑩

⑨ Turn R along the road (150m). After the corner of the field diverge L on the path in the trees (200m). Turn L down the track to Parsonage Farm Cottages (150m). Turn R between the cottages (50m) then go through the R field to the crosspath (170m). Turn R.

⑩ Go to the top of the hill (300m).

⑪ Turn R (40m), anticlockwise round the buidings and down the hill (North Downs in the distance) into the valley (800m). Descend the valley path R, cross to the houses (300m) and walk up the drive round the R bend (150m). ✳

⑫ At the bend just before the road, take the path ahead to the next drive (60m). Go R (100m). After the house continue ahead (300m).

⑬ Cross the drive and follow the path between gardens, round the pond and up steps (100m). Turn L. Stay on the same path up round the flank of the hill in the wood (200m) then beside the lane and houses to Witley Lodge (200m).

The words **fauna** and **flora** are often misused. They are not plural nouns for animals and plants but collective nouns. A fauna is the set of animals in a particular area eg the fauna of a pond or a garden or the British Isles. Two islands have two faunas. Flora is used in the same way. The set of bacteria in the body is also refered to as a flora because bacteria were originally considered plants. **Data** is a collective noun in the same way.

25 Witley, Hambledon and Wormley

About 8.4 km/5¼ miles. Confusing heath and wood, undulating, half shady, good in winter. OS maps 1:25000 133 Haslemere, 1:50000 186 Aldershot.

Start at Witley Lodge, SU 945 396, near Witley Church or at Hambledon Church, SU 970 389m, or at the car park near Sweetwater Pond, SU 953 390

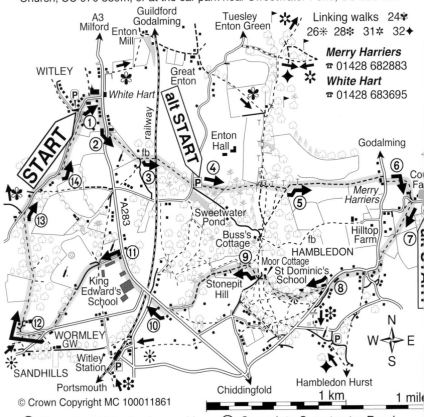

© Crown Copyright MC 100011861

① From the Witley Lodge parking area, walk down the lane past Witley Church to the A283 ❁ opposite the *White Hart* (200m) Follow the pavement R (200m).

② Cross to the recreation ground beside the Chichester Hall. Follow the L edge to the end (300m).

③ Join the track in the wood. Almost immediately (30m) turn L on the footpath down beside the garden, over the footbridge and under the railway (Portsmouth line) (100m). Go on to the road (300m).

④ Cross into Sweetwater Pond car park and carry on up the edge of the wood (450m). At the cross paths, ✦❁ continue past the heath R (Buss's Common) to join the broad oblique track (200m).

⑤ Turn L (60m) and curve R under cables. Go on under trees between fields to the road in Hambledon next to the *Merry Harriers* (700m).

⑥ Cross opposite the pub. Go up the path, round a R bend and along the drive to the next road (300m). (Hambledon Church is 100m up L).

⑦ Cross the road and climb the bank into the field. Go down the oblique path and stay ahead to the house (500m). Walk down the road past the side road L in the village (100m) and on to the gateway of St Dominic's School R (300m). ✳

⑧ After it diverge R up the path to the trees on Hambledon Common. Stay ahead on the heath path round the flank of the hill down to the lower path (400m) then turn R to Moor Cottage (150m). ✳

⑨ Continue over the vehicle track and the bridleway (30m) and up the steep path on Stonepit Hill to the top (200m). Go through the gateway, along the drive past the front of the house (100m), and down the drive to the A283 in Wormley (600m).

⑩ Cross to the pavement and follow the main road down R, over the railway (200m) and up past King Edward's School (300m).

⑪ After the school and houses turn L along the drive beside the sports field (200m). Stay ahead up the bridleway under trees, then up a tarmac drive, to the next road (500m). Follow the road R (60m).

⑫ Over the brow of the hill, soon after the side road (30m), turn R on the heath path which converges on the side road. At the end continue on the road (150m). Just after the footpath L in the trees, turn R up the shared drive. Continue on the path between gardens then through woodland. (Banicle Hill L had a semaphore tower on top). The path descends (500m) then rises to the next road (300m). ✤

⑬ Go down the road R (300m).

⑭ Just after the large house, Hangerfield, watch out for a side path R. Follow it beside the lane down to the next house and keep on down the drive to the parking area at Witley Lodge (500m).

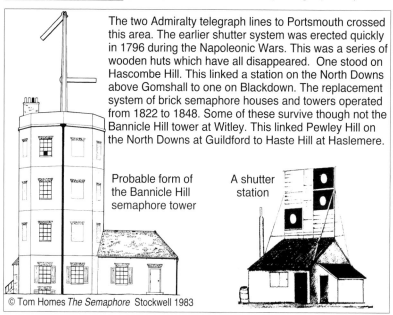

The two Admiralty telegraph lines to Portsmouth crossed this area. The earlier shutter system was erected quickly in 1796 during the Napoleonic Wars. This was a series of wooden huts which have all disappeared. One stood on Hascombe Hill. This linked a station on the North Downs above Gomshall to one on Blackdown. The replacement system of brick semaphore houses and towers operated from 1822 to 1848. Some of these survive though not the Bannicle Hill tower at Witley. This linked Pewley Hill on the North Downs at Guildford to Haste Hill at Haslemere.

Probable form of the Bannicle Hill semaphore tower

A shutter station

© Tom Homes *The Semaphore* Stockwell 1983

26 Chiddingfold and Sandhills

About 9.6 km/6 miles with an extension of 1.8 km/1 mile to Brook. Undulating farmland and woodland mostly on the Weald Clay; muddy in wet seasons; half shady. OS maps 1:25000 133 Haslemere, 1:50000 186 Aldershot.

Start beside Chiddingfold village green, SU 961 354. Parking at Witley Station is free at weekends. On the extension, park opposite the pub at Brook, SU 930 380.

Linking walks 18☆ 24✤ 25✳ 27✦ 28◇ 29★ 30✲

alt START

Haslemere

Milford · Banacle Common · **GW** · site of semaphore tower · Milford · King Edward's School · BROOK · Dog & Pheasant · Fintry · WORMLEY · GW · Witley Station · SANDHILLS · A286 · alt START · London - Portsmouth railway

✦① Make for the garden wall halfway up the main road edge of Chiddingfold green (100m). Pass R of the pond (50m). Turn R on the road (70m) and L on the track in the trees (70m). Stay ahead: R of the graveyard, up under trees, along the hill (250m), along the road to the R bend (200m), between garden fences (120m), along the top of the field to the far corner (450m) and between fences (120m).

② Turn R across the next drive to the field. Go up the R fence and along the top to the road (300m).

③ Go R on the road over the rise (100m) and down to the T-junction (250m). Turn R to houses (350m).

④ Turn back on the track behind the 1st house L (100m). Go round the bend near the drive and follow the yew hedge up the slope (300m), round a curve then level to the hedge bend R (200m). Stay ahead over the field into the wood (100m), down into the valley to the brick bridge (150m), up the other side still in trees, beside fields R (200m), along the R edge of a field (150m), over the railway lines and the next field into the trees (150m).

The Crown
☎ 01428 682255
The Swan
☎ 01428 684688
Dog & Pheasant
☎ 01428 682763
Winterton Arms
☎ 01428 776151
Treacles Tea Shop
☎ 01428 684859

N W E S

© Crown Copyright MC 100011861

⑤ Follow the path down R (60m). Go R in the valley (70m), round L over the bridge and up to the side path L at the brow (150m).

ⓔ *Extension of 1.8 km/1 mile: Turn L across the footbridge. Go up the wood to the field (100m), along the edge and over, R of the garden, to the road (400m). L a bit go up the path and track to the tarmac drive (200m). Descend to the road (50m).*

(f) *Walk down the road L (200m). Turn R along the 2nd side path at the garden hedge, and enter the cricket field at Brook (200m).* ☆

(g) *Climb to the top corner (200m). Go into the trees (20m) and R up the flank eventually over the brow curving R up to the field (200m).* ✤

(h) *Turn R on the path, GW, round the fields to the road (550m).*

(i) *Go L (60m) & R down Bannacle Hill Road past Sebastapol Lane R (250m).* ✳ *At the next footpath R, GW (150m), drop to the next road, avoiding the R branch (100m).* ➤(7)

(6) Stay ahead (150m), up though fields (400m) and up the unmade road at Sandhills to the diverging, concrete drive L (50m). Turn R into the field and make for the top gate in (100m). Turn R down the road (200m).

(8) Outside the station go R parallel with the railway (Portsmouth line) through the car park and along the lane (150m). Turn L on the path past the cottage. Stay ahead beside the wood to more houses, over the access road at the industrial estate (350m) and into the field (100m).

(9) Keep on to the corner (100m) then cross the road and the narrow field into Minepit Copse (40m). Follow the path through the trees into a field (250m). Cross obliquely to the footbridge at the middle of the far side (200m). Stay ahead to the corner of the next field (120m). Outside, go L on the grass track (50m) and R up into the field.

(10) Aim ½L out of the corner and curve R round the slope down to the gateway (150m). Cross the narrow field and stream into the wood (30m) and go on up to more fields (150m). Go up the R edge (350m) and ahead to the road near the houses (150m).

(11) Walk down the road L (50m) Immediately after the side road L turn L on the path in the trees and descend to the field (150m). Cross to the bottom corner (100m). ☆

(12) Outside, cross the little brook and turn back R up the adjacent field across to the corner R of the houses (200m). Continue on the track to the road (100m). Turn L on the pavement (50m) and R up Coxcombe Lane (100m).

(13) Take the path next to the house L on the crest of the rise. At the track keep on past the houses and the cricket field to the A283 (250m).

(14) Follow the pavement R to the village green (200m) and cross to the bottom edge (100m). ✳

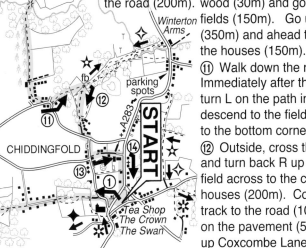

(7) Join the track diverging R from the road R beside the garden fence to a house L (250m). Stay ahead to the cross track (350m). Turn R (100m). Go round the L bend to Witley Station and cross the footbridge (100m).

53

27 Chiddingfold and Frillinghurst

About 7.4 km/4½ miles. Woodland and pasture on the Weald Clay. half shady. Avoid in wet seasons. OS maps 1:25000 133 Dorking 1:50000 186 Guildford.

Start from Chiddingfold village green; park at the bottom edge, SU 961 454.

Linking walks   23✳   26✦   29✳   30★

The Crown ☎ 01428 682255
The Swan ☎ 01420 684688
The Mulberry ☎ 01428 644460
Tea Shop ☎ 01428 684859

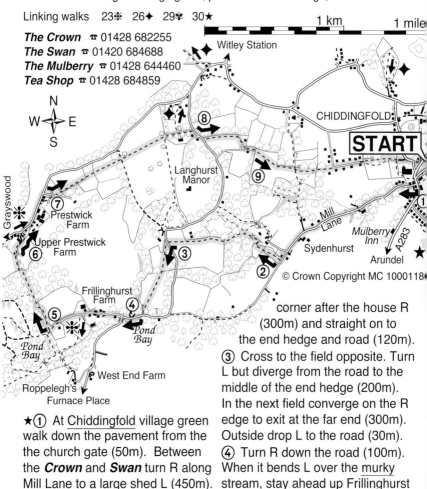

© Crown Copyright MC 1000118

★① At Chiddingfold village green walk down the pavement from the the church gate (50m). Between the **Crown** and **Swan** turn R along Mill Lane to a large shed L (450m). Continue up between fields (450m). past the large house, Sydenhurst L and past the side road R at houses (150m) to the next field R (60m).

② Walk through the field diverging slightly from the R edge to the trees at the end (200m). Turn R into the wood (40m). Go L down to a brook (50m) and up to the field (120m). Go up the R edge to the-entrant

corner after the house R (300m) and straight on to the end hedge and road (120m).

③ Cross to the field opposite. Turn L but diverge from the road to the middle of the end hedge (200m). In the next field converge on the R edge to exit at the far end (300m). Outside drop L to the road (30m).

④ Turn R down the road (100m). When it bends L over the murky stream, stay ahead up Frillinghurst drive past several houses to the fields (300m) ✳ and the house on top, Frillinghurst Old Manor (150m). Carry on beside the R field into Frillinghurst Wood (60m).

⑤ Turn R outside the field. The path follows the edge sometimes in the field sometimes outside. Keep on past the end of the field (200m), and a side path L (50m) to the next

54

field (200m) and up the R edge to the gate near a garden and summer house (100m).

⑥ Exit R on the path round outside the field to the barn L (100m). Stay ahead on the path next to the field then round the pond L to the road (80m). Follow the road R, past barns and cottages (350m).

⑦ After the end cottage, turn R on the drive (80m). At the footpath enter the L field and cross obliquely to the hedge-corner (40m). Stay ahead, L of the hedge, to the end (200m) and continue over the fields, about 80m R of the road, to the row of trees at a path on the rise (300m). ❋ Cross the wide field ahead to the trees at the far edge, L of the sheds (350m). Follow the onward path in the trees and keep on to the road (200m).

⑧ Turn R on the road. Walk over the rise past the Langhurst drive and down. Watch out for the field access above L (100m). Follow the fence along the top (220m) and ½R down to the house drive (80m). Cross to the next drive (20m) and turn L outside the garden (70m).

⑨ Carry on in the field, diverging from the L edge to the re-entrant corner 70m out (200m). Go on round the top edge, over a footpath and into the corner (300m). Stay ahead past gardens (120m), along the road with houses (200m) and on the path down through trees to Chiddingfold (250m). At the bottom continue on the track to the road (70m). ❀ Turn R on the pavement to the bend (60m) then bear L of the pond. Cross the A283 and village green (100m).

Wealden Iron-Making

The first British blast furnace was built at Buxted in Sussex in 1496 for army ordnance. The Weald was the largest iron-producing area in Roman and medieval times. The industry spread into Surrey with furnaces at Dunsfield, Imbhams, West End and Witley. The chief ore was siderite nodules, $FeCO_3$, mined in the Weald Clay. The fuel and reducing agent was charcoal made from coppiced timber. Incomplete combustion made carbon monoxide which took oxygen from the siderite.

Blast furnaces were brick columns packed with mixed ore and charcoal. Air was blasted through from bellows worked by mills to reach 1560°C, the temperature required to melt iron. If smelting was interrupted the furnace had to be rebuilt so mill ponds had to be large for reliability. A *campaign* lasted for months, with charcoal and ore being fed in and iron and slag tapped off. The iron was *cast* in moulds, *sows*, with side arms, *pigs*. The pig iron was sold on for refining.

Earlier furnaces were bloomeries. Ore and charcoal were mixed and encased in clay. Air was pumped in by hand or treadmill but the temperature was not high enough to melt iron. Slag was run off but the solid iron had to be broken out. This was a *bloom*, a network of iron with trapped slag. The bloom was heated and hammered to squeeze out the slag and burn off carbon dissolved in the iron. The product was *wrought* iron.

Hammers of 3 - 4 kg were worked by hammer mills that also drove bellows and machinery like hoists and lathes for gun barrels. Valleys were dammed to make pond bays for large hammer ponds. Some no longer hold water but the earthworks show their sizes. Peak output was about 12,000 tons in 1574.

Coal could not be used for smelting because of its sulphur content. In 1709 Abraham Derby in Shropshire discovered coke could be used and smelting moved to coal mining areas.

28 Hambledon Hurst and Chiddingfold

About 8.9 km/5½ miles with an extension of 1.9 km/1¼ mile to Chiddingfold village green. Heath, wood and farmland, Greensand and Weald Clay. Avoid the Hurst in wet seasons. OS 1:25000 133 Haslemere, 1:50000 186 Aldershot.

Start from Hambledon cricket green, SU 963 380. There are parking spots opposite the Winterton Arms. At weekends parking is free at Witley Station. The extension has parking on the bottom of Chiddingfold village green, SU 961 354.

Linking walks 24✻ 25❊ 26◇ 29✪ 30✻ 32◇ 39✿

Winterton Arms ☎ 01428 776151   ***Treacle's   Tea Shop*** ☎ 01428 684859 ***The Crown*** ☎ 01428 682255   ***Hambledon Shop*** (&

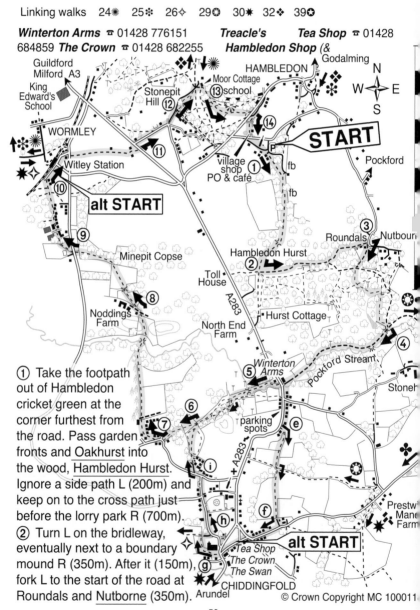

① Take the footpath out of Hambledon cricket green at the corner furthest from the road. Pass garden fronts and Oakhurst into the wood, Hambledon Hurst. Ignore a side path L (200m) and keep on to the cross path just before the lorry park R (700m).

② Turn L on the bridleway, eventually next to a boundary mound R (350m). After it (150m), fork L to the start of the road at Roundals and Nutborne (350m).

© Crown Copyright MC 100011

56

③ Turn R between the garden and field (150m). In the trees, fork R to the bridleway. Slightly R, stay ahead on the small path, round several slight L bends, eventually converging on a gill (stream) to a cross path (300m). Turn R across the gill. Keep on up the slope, over the highest point (100m) and down to the fence near the pond (80m). Follow the fence down L and turn R to the Pockford Stream (100m).❂✤

④ Turn R over the horse bridge. Continue along the valley, past a side bridge L (200m) ✳ to the A283 at the **Winterton Arms** (700m).

ⓔ *Extension of 1.9 km/1¼ mile: Go L on the pavement (300m). At the start of the R curve take the path L between gardens. Continue up the L edge of fields (300m), over the path, L of the hedge ahead and straight on to the road (400m).* ✳

ⓕ *Go down the road R and down the green to the **Crown** (450m).*

ⓖ *From Chiddingfold village green cross into the churchyard. Pass L of the church (100m) and turn R on the path across to the track outside (100m).✥ Turn R to the road (70m).*

ⓗ *Follow the pavement L (400m).*

ⓘ *Turn L on Woodside Road (30m) and R on the track under the trees (150m). Cross the field diagonally to the far corner (200m). Outside turn back into the next field L.* ➔⑥

⑤ Take the path opposite the pub to the bridge on the murky stream (200m). Keep on between fields. The path splits and rejoins. At the end cross into the R field (450m).

⑥ Diverge from the L fence up to the middle of the far edge (100m) and carry on up the path through the trees (150m).

⑦ Go R, up the road (50m) then R up the path, past gardens (150m). Carry on at the L edge of the fields (350m), down through the wood (200m), over the streams and strip of field (30m), up round the hillock and out at the top L corner (150m).

⑧ Turn L and enter the next field R (50m). Go on to the footbridge (150m). Cross the next field to the far L corner (200m) then follow the path through Minepit Copse and over the field to the road (300m).

⑨ Cross to the field opposite. Go along the fence (100m) and through the trees. Carry on between the industrial estate and houses, along the edge of the wood and past a garden and cottage to the railway (Portsmouth line) (450m). ✳❄

⑩ Turn R to Witley Station and continue round to the T-junction (200m). Slightly R cross Combe Lane and take the path between gardens to the A283 (500m).

⑪ Cross slightly L (30m) and walk up Wormley Lane to the R bend (300m). Continue up the track between drives (100m)

⑫ Turn R up the steep side path beside a garden and immediately L up the bank into the trees. Over the brow, follow the heath path (L) above the sunken track. Rejoin the track before the house (250m). ✤

⑬ Make for the R corner of Moor Cottage and continue up the main path (200m). Just before the top don't bear L up the cross path but continue down round the flank of the hill to Hambledon (300m).

⑭ Cross the road to the track and, R of the houses, take the downhill curving footpath to the village shop /café) (150m) and cricket green.

29 Chiddingfold, Hambledon Hurst & Stonehurst

About 8.4 km/5¼ miles with a short cut of 1.2 km/¾ mile. Wood and farmland; undulating; half shady. The paths through the woods are unpleasant in wet seasons. OS maps 1:25000 133 Haslemere, 1:50000 186 Aldershot.

Start in Chiddingfold, parking at the bottom of the village green, SU 961 354.

Linking walks   26★   27❀   28✿   30✦   39♣

Winterton Arms ☎ 01428 76151   **The Crown** ☎ 01428 682255
The Swan ☎ 01428 684688   **Treacle's Tea Shop** ☎ 01428 684859

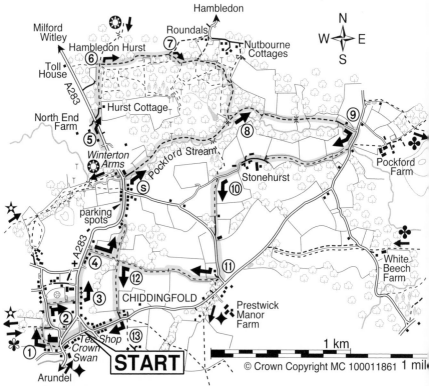

★❀① From the bottom corner of Chiddingfold village green cross into the churchyard. Pass L of the church (100m) and turn R on the path across to the track (100m).

② Go R along the track (70m), L along the road (200m) and R on the path beside the football field to the main road (200m). Cross.

③ Follow the pavement L, past the cricket field (200m) to the path R at the bent drive (150m).

④ Go up the path (250m) and take the side path L across the field. Keep on at R edges then down between gardens to the A283 (300m). Follow the pavements R to the **Winterton Arms** (300m). ✿

Ⓢ *Short cut of 1.2 km/¾ mile: Turn R down the track between the pub and the stream. Stay ahead on the path beside fields (250m), into the wood, down the wooded valley (500m), past a side path R over the*

58

murky stream, to the side path L, 10m after a bridge (200m). ➡⑧

⑤ Continue on the pavement L of the A283 up to the drive of North End Farm L (450m). Cross the road and take the drive to Hurst Cottage (100m). Continue over the grass in front of the house into the wood, Hambledon Hurst, to the cross path just after the lorry yard L (250m).

⑥ Turn R on the bridleway. Watch out for the boundary mound beside the path R. At the end of it (350m) continue to the fork (150m).

⑦ Fork R. Disregard many side turns. The path passes fields (350m) then swings R down to the Pockford Stream (400m). Turn L.

⑧ Carry on along the valley into fields (250m). Stay ahead near the L edge (350m). In the last field aim for the house beyond it (200m) and go out along the track past the house at Pockford (100m). ❖

⑨ Turn back R along the road (150m). Just after the bridge and before the next house, turn R on the path up between the fields (600m). At the top join the track skirting R of the Stonehurst Farm buildings (200m). Continue round the S-bend and up the tarmac drive to the crossing path after the paddocks (200m).

⑩ Turn L into the field. Follow the L edge (250m) and continue down the track and along the road (L), ascending to the next house R, Rystead (250m). ✦

⑪ Turn R across the drive, a little way into the trees (50m) then R along the track to the fields. Go up the L edge (300m). Cross L to the adjacent field but go on in the same direction to the cross hedge (400m).

⑫ Don't go past the hedge but turn L beside it. Stay ahead over the field and down the track to the road at Chiddingfold (400m).

⑬ Walk down the road R (250m) and along the village green.

The English **glass-making industry** started around Chiddingfold. In Egypt glass beads appeared about 1500BC. Glass-blowing seems to have started around 50BC in Palestine. In England the Romans and Saxons had imported drinking vessels of glass. Bede writes of glaziers being brought from Gaul in about 682 for the new monastery at Monkwearmouth. The earliest known glass-man in England was Laurence, *Vitrearium*, de Dunkeshurstlonde (Duns Farm). He appears in a deed of 1226. His name occurs again in 1240 supplying glass when Westminster Abbey was being rebuilt for Henry III. The early makers were all Flemish or French. The glass-industry faded in this area after the use of timber was proscribed in 1620, but spread else-where under the same people.

Sand by itself melts at 1710°C to form silica glass (SiO_2) but this temperature was beyond the early makers. Adding soda or potash (to provide sodium or potassium) turned it into silicate glass (Na_2SiO_4, K_2SiO_4) which melted at lower temperatures. Bracken ash was produced locally for potash. A mixture of ash and sand, 2:1 by volume, was heated in stout clay pots in a wood-fuelled furnace. The sand came from thin outcrops in the Weald Clay and from the Greensand. The district was covered by managed woods, coppiced for fuel. Later, when window glazing started, the little leaded panes were cut from discs up to 60 cm wide made by fast-spinning blown bulbs. Loseley Papers record a fracas between glass-makers in 1569 when a red hot glass-making rod was wielded.

Wealden Glass 1226-1615 S E Winbolt 85pp

30 Chiddingfold and Botany Bay Forest

About 6.8 km/4¼ miles with a forest extension of 3.8 km/2⅓ miles to the Sussex border. A Weald Clay walk; avoid in wet seasons. Lots of shade for summer walking. Mostly level but with short steep slopes at the gills. Lots of stiles. OS maps 1:25000 133 Haslemere, 1:50000 186 Aldershot.

Start in Chiddingfold at the bottom of the village green, SU 961 354.

Linking 26✳ 27★ 28✳ 29✦

The Crown ☎ 01428 682255
The Swan ☎ 01428 684688
Tea Shop ☎ 01428 684859

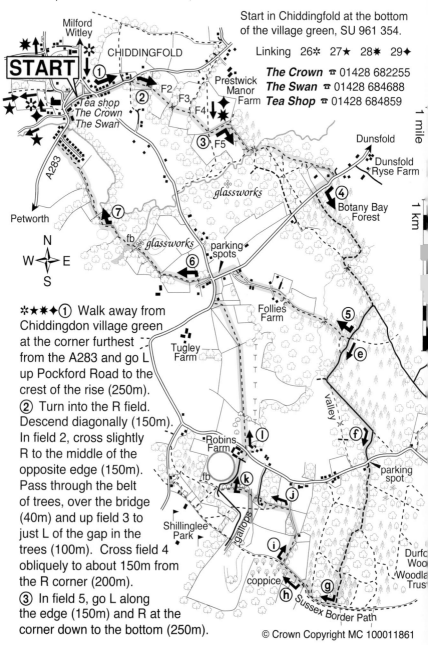

✳★✳✦① Walk away from Chiddingdon village green at the corner furthest from the A283 and go L up Pockford Road to the crest of the rise (250m).

② Turn into the R field. Descend diagonally (150m). In field 2, cross slightly R to the middle of the opposite edge (150m). Pass through the belt of trees, over the bridge (40m) and up field 3 to just L of the gap in the trees (100m). Cross field 4 obliquely to about 150m from the R corner (200m).

③ In field 5, go L along the edge (150m) and R at the corner down to the bottom (250m).

© Crown Copyright MC 100011861

Turn L in the valley over the bridge (20m). Continue in the valley (100m). Disregard several side path R and stay ahead up through the wood to the gardens (350m). Keep on down beside the garden fences to the road (200m).

④ Walk along the road R (200m) and turn L on the Botany Bay forest track. Follow it to a broad curve (500m), round R then L, down over a murky stream (200m) and up to a 3-way track junction (300m). Turn R on the hard track. Watch out for a crossing footpath (300m).

ⓔ *Extension of 3¾ km/2⅓ miles to the Sussex border: Stay on the track (300m), round a L bend at the edge of a valley and on (500m).*

ⓕ *Keep to the hard track when it bends ½R (200m). Cross the road and continue, L of the house, on the forest track (450m). At the unequal fork keep to the main track R, curving L, to the edge of the forest, outside fields (550m).*

ⓖ *Turn R. Follow the boundary path L into the dip (250m).*

ⓗ *Don't go up to the R field but cross the boundary L (10m) and go on beside it (Sussex Border Path) over a rise to the coppice (150m). Walk down the edge briefly (60m) then turn R into the adjacent field.*

ⓘ *Cross the end of the field (200m) and go L down the drive from the house (200m).*

ⓙ *Turn L into the field. Keep to the R edge (150m) and stay ahead R of the garden to the drive from the house (80m). Cross to the pond and pass R of it into the field (40m). Cross the gallops and follow the hedge to the end of the shallow R bulge (200m).*

ⓚ *Turn R through the hedge and cross to the track (40m). Follow the track R to Robins Farm (200m). Cross the track from the stables and pass R of the garden to the road (60m). Go L on the road (40m) and into the corner of the field R.*

ⓛ *Go up the field to the middle of the top edge (200m). Carry on at the L edge of the next field (500m). In the next, don't keep to the edge but aim for the house at the middle of the top edge (300m). Cross into the narrow field and aim for the far L corner (70m). Walk along the road R (150m). Go L. ➔⑥*

⑤ Turn R on the side path (50m). Ignore the side path L and go down to the stream, up to the edge of the forest, beside fields, past Follies Farm L (550m) and along the drive (150m). When the drive bends L at barns, stay ahead between hedges and keep on to the road (150m). Turn L along the R verge (200m).

⑥ At the road junction go up the tarmac drive to the garden gate (100m). Turn R through the hedge (15m). Follow the L edge round the fields, undulating to the wooded corner (500m). Go down through the trees and over footbridges at the pond (50m) then R up the stepped path to the field (80m). Carry on beside the wood (150m).

⑦ Before the end of the wood turn R down through the trees (50m). Continue on the path at the edge of the fields soon rising (200m). Just before the top of the L field drop down the bank R (10m) but keep on in the same direction (100m). Pass behind gardens to the A283 (200m). Follow the pavement R to Chiddingfold village green (300m).

31 Hydons Heath and Tuesley

About 8.7 km/5½ miles. Farmland, heath and woods on the Greensand; half shady, short steep climbs. If starting from Ashstead Lane, a short cut of 1.0 km/²⁄₃ mile can be made and combined with the extension of 500m/¹⁄₃ mile. OS maps 1:25000 145 Guildford + 133 Haslemere 1:50000 186 Aldershot.

Start at Hydons Ball car park, SU 978 402, or, on the extension, at the kerbside in Ashstead Lane, SU 968 425.

Linking walks 24✱ 25✱ 32☆ 35✱

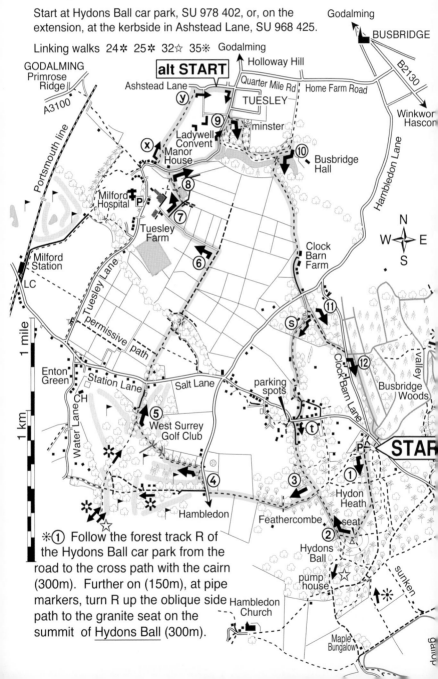

※① Follow the forest track R of the Hydons Ball car park from the road to the cross path with the cairn (300m). Further on (150m), at pipe markers, turn R up the oblique side path to the granite seat on the summit of Hydons Ball (300m).

② Turn R (W) across the flat top away from the Octavia Hill granite seat and trig point (40m) and down to the path with fence crossing the hill (80m). ☆ Descend R to the cross path (350m). Turn L.

③ Follow the path down round the hillside past coppice and between fields to the road (900m). ❈

④ R of the track on the other side, take the path to the golf course. Go between golf mounds and cross into the trees (150m). Turn L along the fence to the corner of the field (300m). Take the path ½R through the trees. Pass R of the mound. Cross the junction of golf tracks (100m) and the next fairway to the path in the belt of trees (200m).

⑤ Turn R through the trees to the house (80m). Stay ahead: down the drive (200m), over the road, along the path L of the garden (100m) and through Tuesley Fruit Farm to more trees (250m). Turn R (30m) then L through the trees over the valley (100m). Turn L to the track junction (30m) then R (original direction) on the track to the farm road L with farm buildings visible in the distance (500m).

⑥ Follow the farm road L (450m).

⑦ Before the buildings, turn R on the slightly curving track (150m) then L on the path between hedge and reservoir down to the road at Tuesley Manor House (200m).

ⓧ *Extension of 500m/⅓ mile: Go L up the road (100m) and R on the path beside the next house. Cross a small valley and ascend between fields to the road (600m).*

ⓨ *Go R on Ashstead Lane (300m), R down Tuesley Lane, past a side road and L into the field (200m).*➜⑨

⑧ Follow the road down R to two side paths R after the pond in the valley (450m). Take the uphill path rising above the road to the field and the main exit gate (200m).

⑨ Outside the gate see Ladywell Convent over the road. Inside, walk away from the road to the shrine at Tuesley Minster (100m). Turn R through the trees curving L to the brow of the hill (150m). Go along the path L above the slope, through a gateway and outside the field (250m). Avoid a branch path L and descend ahead curving L to the T-junction in the valley (100m).

⑩ Go R down the valley path (100m), round the R bend, L across the valley between Busbridge Lakes (200m) and up to Clock Barn Farm (650m). Continue on the drive to the road (250m) and up the drive opposite (150m).

ⓢ *Short cut of 1.0 km/⅔ mile: After the L house, take the side path L. Stay ahead at R edges to the cabin (450m). Go round it, R, L, and ahead at L edges. Continue along the drive to the road (250m).*

ⓣ *Turn R on the road (10m) and L up the shared drive past all the houses (150m). Stay ahead up to the major cross path at a fence corner (350m). Turn R.*➜③

⑪ Before the L house bear L on the bridleway up to the road (400m). Cross slightly R into Busbridge Woods (private woodland but used by walkers and riders) (50m).

⑫ Turn R on the first side track. At the end (500m), go round the corner of the wood L to the exit path (60m) and turn R across the road through trees into the Hydons Ball car park (60m).

32 Hydons Ball and Hambledon

About 8.1 km/5 miles with a short cut of 1.7 km/1 mile. Heath, fields and woods on the Greensand, good in winter and summer, half shady, hilly, good views. OS maps 1:25000 133 Haslemere +145 Guildford, 1:50000 186 Aldershot.

Start at Hydons Ball National Trust car park, SU 978 402, or at Hambledon, from the church, SU 970 389, or the *Merry Harriers*.

Linking walks 24❀ 25✦ 28❖ 31☆ 35✳ 37❀

The Merry Harriers ☎ 01428 682883

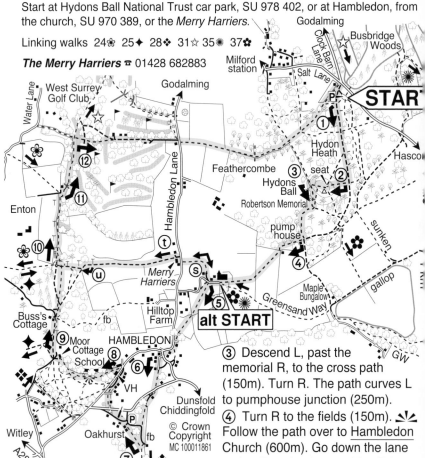

③ Descend L, past the memorial R, to the cross path (150m). Turn R. The path curves L to pumphouse junction (250m).

④ Turn R to the fields (150m). ⬈ Follow the path over to Hambledon Church (600m). Go down the lane to the diverging house drive R just after Court Farm drive (100m).

Ⓢ *Short cut of 1.7km/1 mile or detour to pub: Bear R on the drive and continue down the path, round L, to the **Merry Harriers** (300m). Return ➤⑤ or* ⓣ *Take the track R of the pub between fields (700m).*

ⓤ *Soon after the L bend into the wood (70m), turn R on the major branch track (200m) and R again at the wide straight cross path.* ➤⑩

✳① Take the forest track from the road R of the Hydon Ball car park. Pass the cross path with the cairn (300m) and a ½R rising side path (150m) to the highest point (200m).

② Turn R up the side path to the top of Hydons Ball (200m). ⬈ ❀ Go straight across the flat top (W) away from the Octavia Hill seat and trig point and down to the path and fence which cross the hill (100m).

⑤ Don't go on down the lane but up the bank L into the field. Walk down the middle to the furthest corner. Keep on down to the house (500m) then down the road (100m).
⑥ Turn L at the junction, fork R on the lane past the housefronts and continue down the path to the road (250m). Cross. Take the diverging path past the front of the house and carry on round L to the track (300m). Go L to the drive (100m). ❖
⑦ Turn R past Oakhurst to the cricket green (200m). Cross to the shop (200m). Go up the path L of it (150m) and along the unmade road with houses, past the village hall L, to the road (130m).
⑧ Cross and go L up the slanting footpath outside the school through the trees to the heath. Keep to the main path round the flank of the hill to join the lower path (400m). Turn R to Moor Cottage (150m). ❀✦
⑨ Cross the vehicle track (30m) and turn R on the diverging bridle-way in the trees, gently descending at the foot of the hill to Buss's

Cottage (300m). Don't go down the drive but fork R. Don't take the 1st L (40m) (back to the drive), but bear L at the next fork and diverge R on the public footpath down through Buss's Common to the cross path and power cables in trees (300m).
⑩ Stay ahead into the field (100m), over to the corner of the wood (100m) and past the pond along the edge of the trees (250m).
⑪ Just before the cross track take the side path R of the house (50m). Cross the brook. Go up the edge of the hill in the trees (200m) and down the edge of golf course to the cross path (150m). ☆
⑫ Turn R on the path past the barn and houses (300m) to the road (400m). Cross slightly R and take the track between fields (400m) up into the wood (Feathercombe on the hillside) to the fence corner R at the cross path down from Hydons Ball (400m). Carry on to the 3-way split (100m) and take the middle path to the road next to Hydons Ball car park (500m).

Trig points give joy to walkers and status to hills. They were built for the third triangulation of Great Britain which the Ordnance Survey initiated in 1936 and were adjudged redundant in 1990 when global positioning was thought as accurate as traditional surveying. About 6500 were constructed. Most English ones are tapered square pillars of local stone or concrete. The fundamental mark is a brass stud set in a concrete block a metre below the pillar and there is another in the bottom of the pillar. The brass spider on top is for fixing instruments.

In triangulation, angles from two points, accurately sighted on a third, allow its position to be calculated by trigonometry, hence trigonometric survey and trig point. Sightings were made at night using lamps. In the 1950s trig points were painted white for aerial surveying.

Gibbet Hill (Hindhead) trig point (1938) was used in the primary triangulation over distances of 50 km/30 miles. Hydons Ball trig point (1952) was secondary with triangles of 8km/5 miles. The first triangulation started in 1784 from a base line which now ends at Heathrow.
Ordnance Survey - map makers to Britain since 1791 T Owen & E Pilbeam OS 1992

33 Thorncombe and Nurscombe

About 7.9 km/5 miles through tranquil Greensand country; hilly, in and out of the combes. The paths are well shaded. The views are better when the leaves are off the trees. OS maps 1:25000 145 Guildford, 1:50000 186 Aldershot.

There is no large parking place. Start in Thorncombe Street lay-by, SU 999 421.

Linking walks 8☆ 34❖ 40✳ 41✿ 42✦

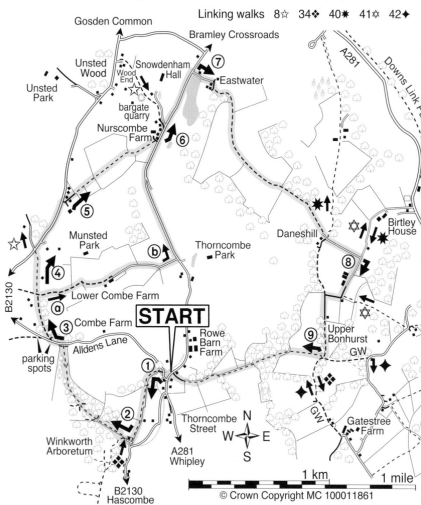

© Crown Copyright MC 100011861

① From the Thorncombe Street lay-by go down the road (60m) and take the 1st R (60m). After the bridge turn L on the track in the trees (50m). Skirt round the bottom edge of the fields to Phillimore Cottage (600m) and cross the end of the garden (20m).

② Turn R along the drive past the cottage (30m). Continue on the footpath (40m). Cross into the field and follow the edge L to the wood (200m). Carry on up the R side of the coomb (350m), over native Bargate on the edge of the plateau and continue to the road (250m).

③ Walk up the road L (100m) and take the bridleway R, below the garden, round the top of the field to the 4-way path junction (300m).
ⓐ *Alternative 450m/¼ mile longer: Take the path R between the fields down the ridge to Lower Combe Farm (500m) and continue down the drive to the road (500m).*
ⓑ *Walk along the road L past Nurscombe Farm L (800m).* ➔⑥
④ Stay on the path ahead down to the road (300m). ☆ Go R down the road past the Munstead Park drive to the next houses R (400m).
⑤ Turn R on the shared drive. Go round the bend and on past all the houses then between fields, eventually descending into the combe. Join the road outside Nurscombe Farm (800m). Turn L.
⑥ Stay on the road, past the houses, down to the end of the large pond R (500m). The large house up L is Snowdenham Hall.
⑦ Turn R along the Eastwater drive. When it bends to the house (150m) take the track R round the barns (70m) and L up out of the combe. Continue between fields up to the house, Daneshill (1300m). ✳
Carry straight on down the drive to the T-junction (300m). ✿
⑧ Turn R up the farm drive. Keep on past the barns R (300m) to the house L, round the R bend to the top (100m) and L to the next house, Upper Bonhurst (200m). Continue on the bridleway in the trees to the next junction (250m). ❖✦
⑨ Turn R between fields, out of the trees, and almost immediately R again into the field. Bear L up the steepest part of the slope to the nearest part of the wood (200m).

Continue up through the trees (250m) into the field on top, level along the R edge (250m) and down the edge of the hill under trees; the path is sunken near the bottom (250m). Outside the fields, descend to the road L of a house in Thorncombe Street (100m).

A **combe** or coomb is a valley set in a hillside. The word, a Celtic remnant, is part of *Com*pton and Welsh place names with *Cwm*. Here, Nurscombe, Thorncombe, Hascombe, Binscombe and Farncombe lie below the plateau of the calcareous Bargate sandstone. As it overlies softer Lower Greensand strata the escarpment and valleys are steep and calcium improves the soils below. Bargate is the pleasant brown stone of the old houses in the district. The origin of the name is unknown

The Greensand follows the lie of the chalk all around the Weald but only in this area does it have Bargate. The best quarries make the craggy skyline above Godalming. Large blocks were levered out, *doggers*, and cut up for building, sometimes to mimic bricks. Another peculiarity of the district is the galetting of Bargate walls where small ironstone chips are inserted in the pointing to protect the mortar.

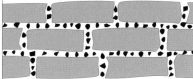

Further from Godalming, the stratum is composed of smaller stones as seen in craggy roadsides. In walls, it is uncut, irregular and more crumbly.

The use of stone declined around the time lorries arrived; so, if ordinary garden walls are stone, it must have been available close by and easy to obtain. Some of the hillsides will have been scarped by stone collectors.

34 Winkworth and Thorncombe Street

About 8.5 km/5⅓ mile with an extension of 1.6 km/1 mile. Hilly farmland and bluebell woods on the Lower Greensand. In Winkworth Arboretum you should keep to the public footpath unless you are a National Trust member or have paid. OS maps 1:25000 145 Guildford, 1:50000 186 Aldershot.

Start from Winkworth Arboretum (10am opening), SU 989 412, or from the lay-by in Thorncombe Street, SU 999 421. On the extension, from the parking area opposite the *White Horse* in Hascombe, TQ 001 394.

Linking walks 33❖ 35✿ 36✿ 38✳ 40✱ 41★ 42✿

The White Horse
☎ 01483 208258
Winkworth Tea Room NT
☎ 01483 208265

① From Winkworth Arboretum car park, L of the house, go along the straight track to the 3-way split on the brow of the hill (250m), down the middle path, past a side path (70m) and down the steps (40m).

68

ⓜ *NT members - to avoid road: Turn L down to the grassy bowl and go L round the edge (250m*

ⓝ *At the bottom turn L. After the rise (100m), diverge R on the side path. Keep on above the bank to the field (300m).*❖ *Outside it turn R and pass the cottage (70m).* ↣④

② Keep on down to the grassy bowl and R of it to the bottom (200m). Turn R (40m) and L round the end of Rowes Flash (lake) to the road (300m).

③ Go L on the road to the R bend (450m) and L up the drive (30m). ❖

④ At Phillimore Cottage take the public footpath across the end of the garden (50m). Stay ahead at the R edge of the fields (550m). In the 3rd field, exit at the gate to the road in <u>Thorncombe Street</u> (50m).

⑤ Go R to the junction (70m) then L (80m). Turn up the track beside the house R (100m). Go on up the hill under trees (250m), over the flat top between fields to the wood (250m), down through the trees to the field (250m) and straight down the spur of the hill (200m). ❋★

⑥ Outside the bottom hedge, turn R up the bridleway, the <u>Greensand Way</u>, to the tarmac lane (600m). ✪

⑦ Opposite Gatestreet Farm L, go R on the drive through the field to the shed L (350m). Keep on to the rising cottage drive R (100m).

⑧ Bear R up the grass. Aim past the corner of the garden to the walkers' gate in the trees halfway up (200m). Cross the track and drop to the valley. Go round the bend up to the field (150m). Cross the top parallel with the R edge and enter the wood (200m). Go round the R edge to the road (600m). ❀❋

⑨ Turn R to the bend (40m) then L up the track (200m) and round the R bend more steeply (130m). ✪

ⓔ *Extension of 1½ km/1 mile to* <u>Hascombe</u> *and the White Horse: Take the side path L (250m), then the first side path R to the shed L (300m). Soon after it, diverge R down the footpath, eventually between houses (250m). Carry on along the lane (250m). Pass R of the pond and L of the church to the B2130 and pub (100m).*

ⓕ *Opposite the **White Horse** take the path between fields (150m) and turn R on the cross path between fields (200m). At the end, fork down R to the wall (25m). Turn R down the drive from Hoe Farm (80m).*

ⓖ *Climb the steps L to the field. Go up the L edge to the top corner (150m). In the next field turn R up through the wood (100m). Take the first side path L, along the bank, and carry on to the end (350m).*

ⓗ *Turn R to the road (80m). Cross and carry on up past Hascombe Court (300m). Keep on ahead along the lane (450m).* ↣⑫

⑩ Stay ahead over the top and down through the trees. Keep on, L of two houses (350m), then wind gently downwards to the 3-way junction near Hascombe (450m).

⑪ Take the bridleway R towards the house (120m). Cross the B2130 and go up the steep track to the top (400m) then follow the lane L to the T-junction (200m). Turn R.

⑫ Keep on to the B2130 (300m).

⑬ Turn R along the main road (150m). Just over the brow of the hill turn off L between drives on the footpath outside Winkworth Arboretum to the car park (550m).

35 **Hydons Ball, Busbridge Woods & Hascombe**

About 8.5 km/5⅓ miles with extensions of 900m/½ mile and 800m/½ mile. Heath and farmland on the Lower Greensand, hilly with good views. Good in winter despite mud. OS maps 1:25000 133+134+145, 1:50000 186 Aldershot.

Start at Hydons Ball NT car park, SU 979 402, or at Hascombe, opposite the *White Horse*, TQ 001 394. On the extension, park at Winkworth Arboretum, NT.

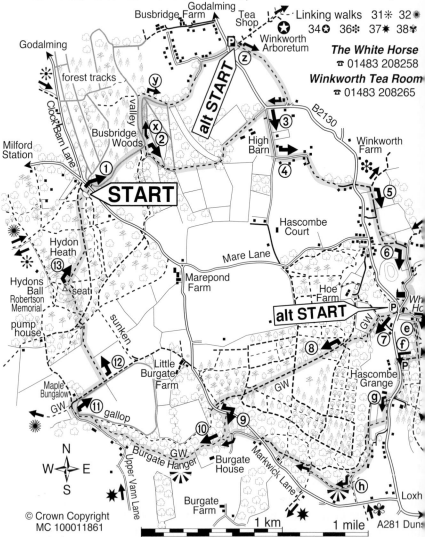

Linking walks 31❋ 32❋
34✪ 36❋ 37❋ 38❋

The White Horse
☎ 01483 208258

Winkworth Tea Room
☎ 01483 208265

© Crown Copyright
MC 100011861

① Within Hydons Ball car park look for the footpath to the road and cross into Busbridge Woods (60m). Go R on the forest track until it bends L into a valley (550m).

ⓧ *Extension of 800m/½ mile: Stay on the main path round the L curve (60m) then diverge R up the rising side track in the trees (250m). Go round the R bend on top.*

70

(y) *Carry on down past the end of the narrow field R (250m), up between fields to the house drives (250m) and along the lane (100m). Turn R on the wider lane to the B2130 (200m). Cross into the car park opposite (60m).* ○

(z) *At Winkworth Arboretum take the path R of the house in the car park, outside the arboretum and past gardens, to the B2130 (550m). Go R up the road to side lane opposite the R bend (150m).* ➔③

② Take the path R. Disregard the next side path R (80m) and stay ahead up under trees all the way to the houses and the B2130 (1100m). Don't join the road. Turn R.

③ Follow the side lane towards Hascombe Court (350m).

④ Take the 1st side lane L to the end (250m). Go round the R bend beside the wall and down to the B2130 (400m). Opposite, take the path to a 3-way junction (100m). ✤

⑤ Turn R (200m). After the house R, stay ahead at the bend (100m). Cut the corner L over the fields or keep on round the L bend (100m) to the house (160m).

⑥ Turn R on the lane, winding round the pond and Hascombe Church to the B2130 junction at the **White Horse** (500m). ✤

(e) *Extension of 1.2 km/¾ mile: Walk up Nore Lane, R of the pub (120m) and turn R on the path beside the shed after the house. Ascend the sunken track (120m). Disregard the uphill track L and carry on through forest (150m).*

(f) *Turn R down the 1st track to the road (150m), L on the path through the car park (150m) then R to the B2130 (100m). Cross ½L (30m).*

(g) *Take the path R above the road (150m), R between fields (150m), L on the track to the bend (50m) and ahead into the wood (350m).*

(h) *After the houses bear L down beside the fence (100m). Turn R on the path above the field (300m).* ✳

↘ *At the end turn R up to the track (50m). Follow it L to the road (400m). Cross and go along the drive of Burgate House (200m). At the end of the L curve take the path up R in the trees to the sunken path (Greensand Way)(50m). Turn L* ➔⑩

⑦ Opposite the pub take the GW path between fields, over a cross path and up into the wood (250m). Fork R steeply up (50m). Carry on less steeply and transfer to the adjacent bridleway R rising to the junction on the brow (100m).

⑧ Stay ahead on the bridleway, GW, over the plateau (800m) and down to the road (200m).

⑨ Walk down the road L (100m) and take the GW path R (150m).

⑩ Stay on the path along the foot of Burgate Hanger (100m) past Burgate House L ↘ until adjacent to the lane L (800), then bear R up the path in the trees to the brow outside the gallop (100m). Keep on to the 4-way junction (150m). ✳

⑪ Turn R, past Maple Bungalow, up the track between fields (300m).

⑫ Take the 1st L, between fields, bending ½R beside trees to a cross track (400m). Don't turn here. Go up to the next cross track (10m) then turn: R (50m), L (50m) & R up onto Hydons Ball (200m). ↘ ✳

⑬ Behind the Octavia Hill seat bear R on the path in the groove down to the vehicle track (300m). Descend L to the car park (350m).

36 Hascombe Hill and Scotsland Farm

About 7.4 km/4½ miles. The extension of 2.7 km/1²/₃ miles and short cut of 1.3 km/¾ mile can be used together. Hilly woods and fields on the Greensand; good views; bluebells. In wet seasons the horse tracks can become very muddy. OS maps 1:25000 133+134+145, 1:50000 186 Aldershot.

Start opposite the *White Horse* in Hascombe, TQ 001 394, or find a parking spot in the village.

Linking walks 34✿ 35❈ 38✾ 38❖ 44✳

The White Horse ☎ 01483 208258

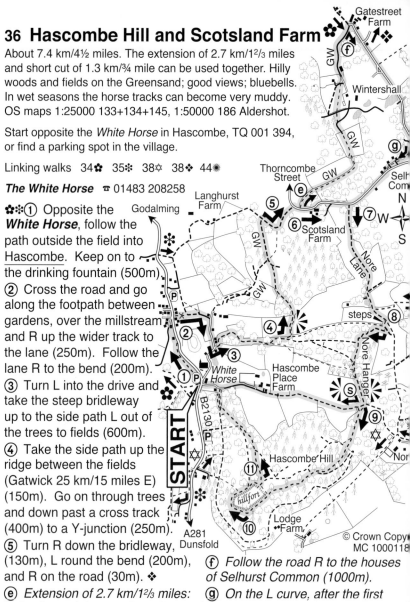

✿❈① Opposite the **White Horse**, follow the path outside the field into Hascombe. Keep on to the drinking fountain (500m)

② Cross the road and go along the footpath between gardens, over the millstream and R up the wider track to the lane (250m). Follow the lane R to the bend (200m).

③ Turn L into the drive and take the steep bridleway up to the side path L out of the trees to fields (600m).

④ Take the side path up the ridge between the fields (Gatwick 25 km/15 miles E) (150m). Go on through trees and down past a cross track (400m) to a Y-junction (250m).

⑤ Turn R down the bridleway, (130m), L round the bend (200m), and R on the road (30m). ❖

ⓔ *Extension of 2.7 km/1²/₃ miles: Take the path L away from the road inside the edge of the wood (500m). Cross the field ahead into a little valley (250m). From the bend in the track go up through the trees to the gate (60m) and down the field. Aim past the garden corner to the drive (200m). The mansion is* Wintershall. *Go L to Gatestreet Farm (400m).*

ⓕ *Follow the road R to the houses of Selhurst Common (1000m).*

ⓖ *On the L curve, after the first house, cut across the grass R and continue up the road past a house L (300m) to the track L (200m).* ➜⑦

⑥ Stay on the road down past Scotsland Farm, over a rise (200m) and down to the bottom of the first field (200m). Turn R on the track.

⑦ Follow the track (Nore Lane) between fields over a rise (500m), down to the pond R (possibly dry) in the dip (200m) ❋✿ and on up to the sunken part of the track below the end of the next field R (200m).

⑧ Climb the stepped path R onto the bank (10m) but don't go up the edge of the field. Follow the path L above the bank (50m) then turn R up the steep winding horse track to the flat top (250m). Disregard the side track R here, and the next (150m), and carry on along the ridge above Nore Hanger, down to the 4-way path junction (300m).

Ⓢ *Short cut of 1.3 km/¾ mile: Turn R on the downhill bridleway (600m). Continue on track and lane down to the White Horse (600m).*

⑨ The bridleway descends R & L. Cross it and bear R to another path (50m). Keep on up Hascombe Hill.

Ignore the diverging path R (150m). Continue on the level at the S edge of the ridge, Dunsfold Airfield far L. Ignore a Downhill side path back L (300m) and a side track (50m). Go on to the start of the hill fort (350m) and the end of the ridge (250m).

⑩ Follow the path as it bends R round the end of the hill (100m) ❋ then curves back along the other side (250m). After another R bend is a path junction at the E end of the hillfort (30m).

⑪ Turn L along the hill immediately diverging on the L path, level then descending. Stay ahead down to the sunken path at the foot of the hill (550m) and bear R down to the end near a house L (100m). Walk down the tarmac Nore Lane to the *White Horse* in Hascombe (120m).

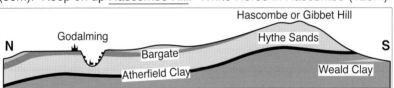

Hascombe Hill and Gibbet Hill are largely composed of Hythe Sands, the Greensand stratum below the Bargate beds, grey jointed stone in seams with sand between. Further east, Leith Hill is part of the same outcrop. The strata were domed as a ripple in the earth's crust caused by the colliding African and Eurasian tectonic plates which pushed up the Alps 60m years ago. Erosion removed the chalk on top leaving the Downs as rough edges.

The Hythe Sands lack calcium and do not retain water so they are covered by heath on hilltops where drainage is greatest. Fields on the northern slopes are more fertile because of the calcareous Bargate sandstone. In worn paths the transition from grey (Hythe) to brown (Bargate) stone is visible.

The lowest division of the Lower Greensand is the Atherfield Clay. It is not hard and does not stand out in valley sides but it causes the springs on the hillsides as water from the sand leaks over its edges. It forms dense clay soils which do not sustain arable agriculture because oxygen is denied to roots and microbes. Where the sand from the hills mixes with the clay, the soil can be very fertile, hence the wheat fields below the escarpment south of the hills.

Greensand is misleading. It was the working title of early geologists for a set of strata later found to be rarely green and with clay in the series. The walking area is on the Lower Greensand; the Upper Greensand here is a chalky sandstone under the Downs

37 Dunsfold and Burgate Farm

About 7.4 km/4²/₃ miles with a hilly extension of 3.2 km/2 miles. Greensand and Weald Clay, undulating. Good for spring flowers, long views, half shady. OS maps 1:25000 133 Haslemere + 134 Crawley, 1:50000 186 Aldershot.

Start at Dunsfold car park on the village green, TQ 006 363.

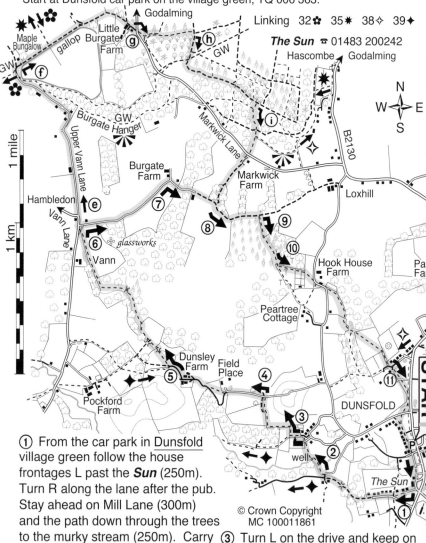

Linking 32✿ 35✳ 38◇ 39✦

The Sun ☎ 01483 200242

Hascombe Godalming

© Crown Copyright
MC 100011861

① From the car park in Dunsfold village green follow the house frontages L past the *Sun* (250m). Turn R along the lane after the pub. Stay ahead on Mill Lane (300m) and the path down through the trees to the murky stream (250m). Carry on to the next house (150m). ✦✦

② Cross the bridge R (20m). Take the path L beside the stream to the well (150m) and up to Dunsfold Church (100m). Carry on beside the hedge after the lych gate (30m).

③ Turn L on the drive and keep on to the end of the little field (100m). Go R up the edge (60m), L along the bottom of the adjacent field (150m) and up R over the top to the drive (200m). ↘ The hills ahead are the Greensand escarpment.

74

④ Turn L along the drive to Field Place (300m) and descend to the valley bottom, either straight down the field or down the track L and round the hairpin bend (300m). Follow the track up the other side and between the houses at Dunsley Farm to the field (150m).

⑤ Just before the field at the top, bear R on the track round the edge of the hillside field into the valley-side field (150m). Don't keep to the track across the field but make for the bottom corner and cross the footbridge (150m). Follow the stream (L) along next field (250m) and through the wood (250m) then cross the footbridge and go up the valley side to the field (250m). Stay at the L edge past the house, Vann, to the road (350m).

ildford

ⓔ Extension of 3.2 km/2 miles: Stay ahead up Upper Vann Lane curving past houses (700m) to the sandy track on top (500m). ✿

ⓕ Turn R along the track past Maple Bungalow, ✳ *over the rise and round down past Little Burgate Farm to Markwick Lane (1100m).*

ⓖ Cross to the path in the trees. Diverge L of the road (50m) and turn L up the escarpment (100m). When the path bends L, transfer to the sunken path R and continue up to the level cross track (250m).

ⓗ Turn R. Cross the Greensand Way bridleway on the brow of the hill (150m). Stay ahead (50m) and curve L with the brow. Identify the breakneck path over the edge opposite the broad side path L (350m) but continue on the brow path. Watch out for the next path R over the edge (50m before the next major side track L) (200m).

ⓘ Drop down the steep path, over the forest track to the field (250m)✧ and go down the edge to Markwick Lane (150m). Carry on opposite, past the wall of Markwick Farm and down the track to the T-junction in the trees (400m). Turn L. ➔⑧

⑥ Turn R along the tarmac drive to Burgate Farm (700m).

⑦ At the junction near the house, branch R to pass the large shed R (200m) and continue on the farm track. Disregard the curved side track up L on the S-bend (200m). ✧

⑧ Stay on the main track to the side path R after the conifers at the start of a belt of trees L (350m).

⑨ Turn down the R edge of the field (150m) and carry on through the wood to the next field (200m).

⑩ Follow L edges (200m). In the field before Hook Farm, cross ½R to the road (100m). Turn R. Go round the L bend to the R bend (80m) then into the L field. Follow the L edge round into the next field (250m) and bear L into the dip (70m). Pass R of the pond, up through the trees, to the next field (60m). Aim obliquely L over the rise to the far L corner (250m). Carry on between hedges past another field and out L to the pond and village green at Dunsfold (120m).

⑪ Go round the R edge of the green, over a drive to the side road (350m). Cross and go along the frontages to the car park (250m).

×2

Devil's Coach Horse - a beetle

38 Hascombe and Dunsfold

About 8½ km/5¼ miles with an extension of 1.9 km/1¼ miles. Some steep paths, numerous stiles, fine views, soft sand in summer, half shady, bad mud in wet seasons. OS maps 1:25000 133 + 134 + 145, 1:50000 186 Aldershot.

Start in Hascombe from the parking area opposite the *White Horse*, TQ 001 394, or, on the extension, in Dunsfold from the village green car park, TQ 006 363.

Linking walks 34✳ 36✿
35❀ 37◇ 39★ 44❀

The White Horse ☎ 01483 208258
The Sun ☎ 01483 200242

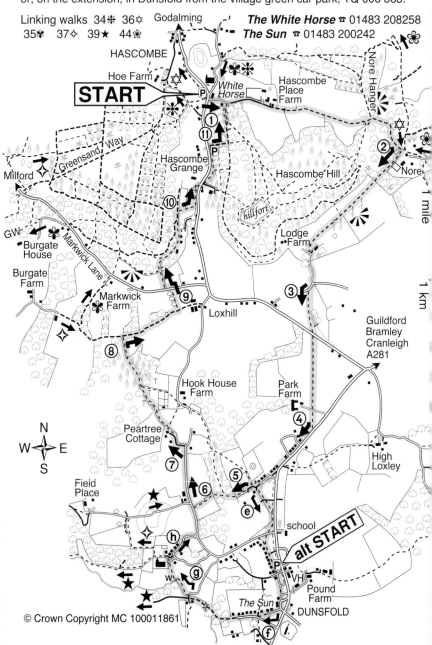

© Crown Copyright MC 100011861

❀☆① Walk up Nore Lane, R of the **White Horse**, past the house and the side path in the cleft R (120m). Continue ahead on the track down past Hascombe Place Farm (350m) to the cottage L (80m) and up the bridleway over the top (650m) ❀.

> ⬓ The valley below is aligned with the notch where the Wey crosses the North Downs at Guildford. In it are the Bramley Wey, the Junction Canal, the Horsham road and the ex-railway.

Stay ahead, steeply down, to the L bend at the next house (300m).

② Go up the path R of the garden, through the trees (300m), along the fields parallel with the top edge ⬓ past Wellingtonias and stone circle and down to the building (700m). Walk down the drive (200m).

③ Turn R on the lane (40m) and L into the field. Descend, R of the ponds, to the nasty road crossing (300m). Continue down the next field (500m). Cross the drive and carry on in the same oblique line to the trees L. Join the road 100m before the houses (150m).

④ Walk along the verge R to the bend (350m) then cut the corner R and follow the lane R of the ponds across the end of Dunsford village green into the corner (200m).

ⓔ *Extension of 1.9 km/1¼ mile to the Sun: Go on round the R edge of the green over the track and side road (450m) then along the house frontages past the car park L (200m) to the **Sun** (300m).*

ⓕ *Turn R along the lane after the pub. At the end continue ahead on the lane (Mill Lane) (350m), down the path through the wood and over the murky stream (250m) to the house L (150m).* ★★

ⓖ *Cross the bridge R (20m) and take the path L beside the stream to the well then up to Dunsfold Church L (250m). Go up the hedge after the lych gate (30m).* ✧

ⓗ *Turn R on the drive. Continue on Church Lane to the T-junction (300m). Turn L (200m).*➜⑥

⑤ Bear R on the track between gardens (30m) then L. Continue into the wood (150m), down and up to the next field (150m) and along the R edge to the road (150m). Turn R.

⑥ Pass the drive of Field Place L to the next house drive L (400m).

⑦ Go up the drive of Peartree Cottage and skirt the lawn to enter the field R of the house (100m). Go along the L edge of the fields (400m), through the wood to the next field and along the L edge to the major farm track (400m). ✿

⑧ Go R along the track to a line of trees L before the buildings (450m).

⑨ Take the path L across the field (140m). Turn L on the road (40m) and R up the escarpment. Ignore side paths and carry on up through the trees (200m). Bear R on the ± level path above houses. Stay ahead down to the fields (350m).

⑩ After the converging track L (50m), turn R down between the fields (150m) and L along the bottom to the road (100m). Cross to the drive (20m L) and take the path parallel with the road to the cross track beyond the car park (250m).

⑪ Go up this track (150m) and L at the foot of Hascombe Hill (150m). Disregard the uphill path R and keep on down to Nore Lane near a house (120m). Descend L to the *White Horse* in Hascombe (120m).

39 **Dunsfold and Pockford**

About 7.4 km/4½ miles. Undulating farmland and woods on the Weald Clay, muddy in wet seasons, excellent for bluebells and other spring flowers.
OS maps 1:25000 133 Haslemere +134 Crawley, 1:50000 186 Aldershot.

Start at Dunsfold car park on the village green, TQ 006 363.

Linking   28✿ 29✿ 37✦ 38★

The Sun ☎ 01483 200242

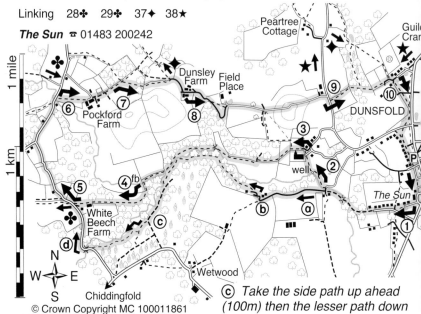

© Crown Copyright MC 100011861

① From the car park in Dunsfold follow the house frontages L to the ***Sun*** (300m). Turn R along the road after the pub. Continue on the path, then on the lane (Mill Lane)(350m). Go on down the track through the wood and over the murky stream (250m) to the house L (150m).

ⓐ *Slightly longer alternative: Go straight on up the track beside the wood (450m).*

ⓑ *At the path junction just after the cottage turn R & L & R on the main track to the next cottage (100m). Just before the garden take the footpath R into the valley (600m). At a L bend in the stream join the forestry track and follow it R near the stream until it bends L up the valleyside (300m).*

ⓒ *Take the side path up ahead (100m) then the lesser path down R. Follow the stream all the way to the next road (400m).*

ⓓ *Go over the bridge and up the road to White Beech (400m).* ✦**⑤**

② Cross the bridge R (20m) and take the path L beside the stream to the well then R up to Dunsfold Church (250m). Go up the hedge after the lych gate (30m).

③ Turn L on the drive. Keep on to the end of the little field (60m). In the next field go down the edge (100m) then along the edge of the wood to the track (150m). Continue in the field at the R edge (200m). When the edge bends R, stay ahead converging on the stream L (100m). Cross the bridge and continue through the wood (400m) then outside a field R (200m).

④ At the end of the field go over the footbridge L and up the valleyside (100m). Follow the path past White Beech Farm (600m) ✤ and turn R on the road.

⑤ Go up over the hill and down to the junction (550m) then R down Vann Lane to the bridge (300m).

⑥ After the bridge enter the field R and cross to the gate at Pockford Farm (250m) or, further on (200m), take the farm drive R (250m). Pass L of the barns to the drive L from the road (30m) and continue ahead on the cart track R of fields. When the track bends R (100m), stay ahead up the footpath at the L edge of the field to the cross path out of the wood halfway up (150m).

⑦ Bear R over the field, halfway up the slope (150m). Continue beside the hillside field to the track from the L field (200m) ✦ and ahead to the downhill track L at Dunsley Farm (150m).

⑧ Walk down the hard track between the houses and barns to the R bend in the valley (200m). Either enter the field ahead and go up the L edge or stay on the track up round the hairpin bend to the top (300m). Continue on the drive, over a rise, to the road (800m). ★

⑨ Turn R on the road (40m) and L into the field. Follow the L hedge to the end (150m). Keep on down through the trees, up the other side (150m), along the track and round the bend R into the corner of the village green at Dunsfold (150m).

⑩ Follow paths near the R edge of the green round to the minor road (450m). Cross to the houses and go on along the frontages to the car park (200m).

Bacteria and viruses are wrongly lumped together as minute pathogens, disease-causers. Bacteria are whole organisms but viruses are not. Both are controlled by vaccines but antibiotics cannot reach viruses inside cells

A virus has a few genes in a protein shell, like a piece of chromosome. It can penetrate the cells of an organism and hijack their metabolism to produce and discharge more viruses: hepatitis flu, rabies, foot & mouth, tulip-break.

A bacterium is a whole organism with a chromosome and metabolism. It has thousands of genes and enzymes to make its components from food and it can reproduce. Bacteria are usually single-celled, spherical or sausage-shaped about $1\mu m$ wide $(= 1/1000$ mm): TB, cholera, botulism, bubonic plague, meningitis, chlamydia, banana wilt.

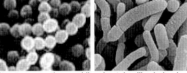

Streptococcus thermophilus Lactobacillus bulgaricus

Viruses are too small be seen by light microscope. TMV tobacco mosaic virus was the first to be imaged, by electron microscope. It is rod-like, 300 x 18 nm. 1 nanometer $= 1/1000$ μm. Viruses have only 4 - 200 genes but vary greatly in structure suggesting different origins. A group called *phage* attack bacteria and appear to inject their DNA like syringes

Phage T4 attacking *Escherischia coli*

There are hundreds of pathogenic species of bacteria but most or them are are harmless. All organisms need vitamin B_{12} which is made only by bacteria. It is probable all organisms depend on specific bacteria in other ways. All ecosystems need bacteria for recycling. Some manufacturing depends on cultivated bacteria.

Viruses are discovered only through disease. They can be used in genetic engineering to convey DNA into cells.

40 Bramley and Lordshill

About 8.9 km/5½ miles. The villages and undulating farmland on the Lower Greensand with a steeper extension of 2.8 km/1¾ mile over Chinthurst Hill; fairly shady. OS maps 1:25000 145 Guildford, 1:50000 186 Aldershot.

Start in Bramley; park at the disused railway station, TQ 010 451, or around the village hall in Hall Road. On the extension start from Chinthurst Hill car park.

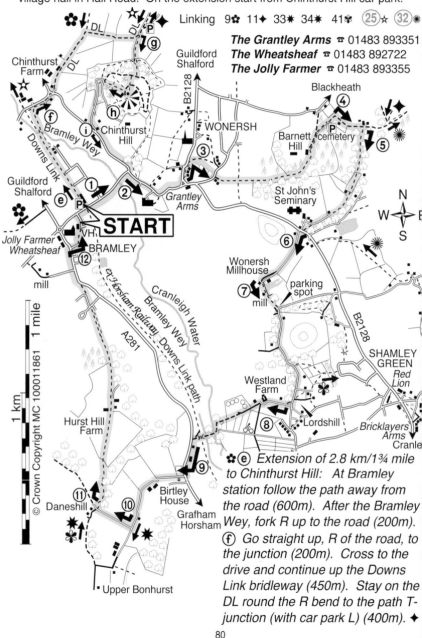

Linking 9♣ 11✦ 33✳ 34✳ 41❀ ㉕☆ ㉜✳

The Grantley Arms ☎ 01483 893351
The Wheatsheaf ☎ 01483 892722
The Jolly Farmer ☎ 01483 893355

❀ⓔ *Extension of 2.8 km/1¾ mile to Chinthurst Hill: At Bramley station follow the path away from the road (600m). After the Bramley Wey, fork R up to the road (200m).*
ⓕ *Go straight up, R of the road, to the junction (200m). Cross to the drive and continue up the Downs Link bridleway (450m). Stay on the DL round the R bend to the path T-junction (with car park L) (400m).* ✦

ⓖ *Walk up Chinthurst Hill. Keep to uphill paths to the tower on top (450m).* ↘↗ *See box Walk 11.*

ⓗ *Behind the tower (opposite the doorway) find the steepest path. Descend (200m) then go down the tarmac drive L to the road (350m).*

ⓘ *Walk down the road L to the next junction (350m) then L.* ➔②

✿① From Bramley Station follow the road away from the village centre over the Bramley Wey and round the R bend (400m).

② Keep on past Wonersh church and along The Street to the Pepper Pot and **Grantley Arms** (450m).

③ Over the road, turn L along the edge of the gardens towards Guildford (150m). When the green widens, follow the hedge round to the next road (150m). Cross slightly R (30m) to the track at the timber-framed house. Go up the path between fields and over Barnett Hill (700m). After the eponymous house (150m), fork R (100m). Continue past the cemetery (70m).

④ Go round the R bend and down the sunken track (200m). ✳

⑤ Opposite the houses turn R down the valley. Pass through small fields and a garden (450m). Stay ahead (200m). After the next house continue down the tarmac drive to the R curve (150m) then take the side path ahead to the B2128 (nasty crossing) (100m).

⑥ Cross slightly R and go down the drive of Wonersh Mill house (300m). Fork R on the parallel track, R of the garden (150m).

⑦ Turn L, along the garden wall, over the millstream and continue to the road (200m). Walk along the road (R) past the knoll L (700m). ✿

⑧ Just before the side road L, where the trees give way to grass at Lordshill Common, turn R along the tarmac drive to Westland Farm (150m). Skirt the buildings and carry on along the track (450m), round bends over the Bramley Wey and the Junction Canal, under the Downs Link (ex-Horsham Railway) and up to the A281 (300m).

⑨ Follow the pavement L (300m). On the curve cross to the first drive opposite. Go up it past the back of Birtley House and on (550m). ✳

⑩ Before the farm buildings turn R up the tarmac drive (300m).

⑪ Just before the house take the path R into the trees. Stay ahead between fields to Hurst Hill Farm (700m), through the woods down to Bramley (700m), along a little road (100m), between houses (100m) and beside the A281 (250m).

⑫ Before the **Wheatsheaf** and the **Jolly Farmer** turn R on Windrush Close (60m) and take the path L to the village hall (200m) or turn R at the next road to the station (100m).

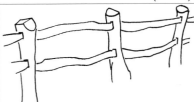

The rustic fences of W Surrey are cut from chestnut, coppiced on a 30 year cycle. The posts are whole or ½ width logs, the rails ¼ or ⅛, split by hammer and chisel. They have now spread to other areas, sometimes with squared oak posts which better resist soil rot. Coppicing survives because the steep Greensand slopes have little other commercial use. In the past coppiced timber was used for making charcoal. John Evelyn estimated Sussex had 200,000 acres of coppice in 1667.

41 Shamley Green, Run Common and Daneshill

About 7.0 km/4⅓ miles with an extension of 1.8 km/1¼ miles. A Greensand walk across the great Wey valley mainly through arable farmland.
OS maps 1:25000 145 Guildford, 1:50000 186 Aldershot.

Start from Shamley Green, parking beside Woodhill Lane near the pond, TQ 032 438, or, when there is no cricket, outside the Arbuthnot Hall.
On the extension start at the Run Common lay-by, TQ 032 419.

Linking walks 33✡ 34★ 40✾ 42✧ 43✿ (32)✦ (33)✦

Red Lion
☎ 01483 892202
Bricklayers Arms
☎ 01483 898377

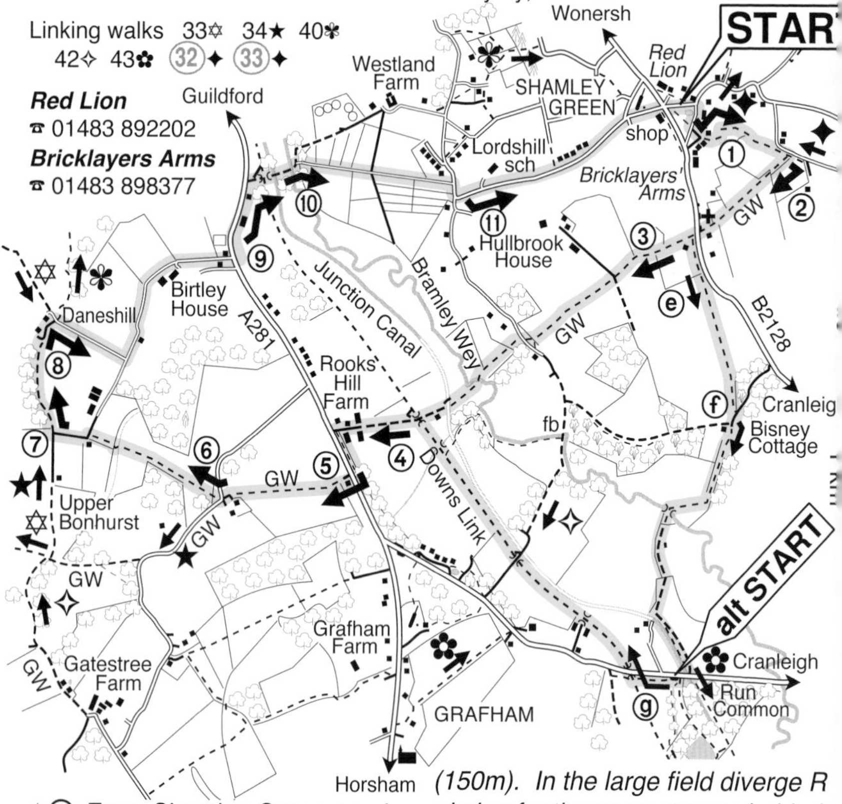

✦① From Shamley Green pond follow the road L of the green half-way to the main road. Bear L on the track, looking out for the path L between houses (100m). Follow it around bends to the field (200m) and up beside the hedge (150m).
② Turn R on the path across the top of the field (Greensand Way). Pass the church and cross the road to the church car park (450m).
ⓔ *Extension of 2 km/1¼ mile: Turn L on the path near the road (150m). In the large field diverge R aiming for the nearest trees behind the highest point. Follow the edge to the track in the trees (450m).*
ⓕ *Turn R (50m). Continue L of the house to the field (250m), ½R to the bridge over the Bramley Wey (Cranleigh Water) (100m) and along the track to a L bend (300m). Soon after the L bend (50m), bear R to the Junction Canal. Keep on and cross the road (200m).* ✿
ⓖ *From the Run Common lay-by take the path L of the road (200m).*

Turn R on the Downs Link path under the old Horsham Railway bridge to the next bridge (550m) and the third (600m). After that ascend L to the farm track. ♦④

③ Stay ahead (GW) between fields, over a farm track (300m) down to a tarmac drive (400m). ♦ Slightly R, find the onward path. Continue down, over the Bramley Wey (200m), ahead to the top of the field (150m) then on the track past a house L and over the old Horsham Railway bridge (100m).

④ Walk down to the A281 through Rooks Hill Farm (300m).

⑤ Turn L along the broad verge near the hedge (150m). Cross and follow the track beside the house, GW. Keep on between fields up past the garden hedge and down the drive to the road (450m). ★✿

⑥ Take the footpath up the bank, opposite. Go through the trees and straight up the R edge of the wood, over the top, past the end of the wood (300m), down to the gate in the valley and up the field R of the house to the track (200m). Pass round the bend, up the track to the trees (100m).✿ Look back over the Wey valley, 2½ km/1½ miles wide.

⑦ At the L bend, turn R up the bridleway in the trees. Keep on to the house, Daneshill (400m). ❀

⑧ Go R down the tarmac drive to the T-junction (300m) then L down past Birtley House (nursing home) to the A281 (600m).

⑨ Cross to the pavement and turn L. Follow the road round the curve and up the rise (300m). Near the top, turn R down the track under the Downs Link path (old Horsham Railway), over the Junction Canal and over the Bramley Wey (200m).

⑩ Don't turn L with the track but climb to the field and pass between paddocks to the next road (550m).

⑪ Turn R on the road (50m). Go round the L bend and on all the way to Shamley Green (800m).

When crossing a cricket field, watch out for 1" buttercups. They, and other lawn weeds, avoid decapitation by keeping their heads down, not through perspicacity but through selection. All offspring have genetic variation and a few will be dwarfs. In normal buttercup terrain these would be killed by shade from taller plants but mowing removes the competition and permits them to flourish. Many cricket fields have been mowed for decades if not centuries.

The very large leaves on the banks of streams and ditches belong to butterbur, *Petasites hybridus*. It is said they were used for wrapping butter. The plant does have flowers but they open in March before the leaves expand so are not seen together. There are other species and coltsfoot is closely related. They are in the daisy family, Asteraceæ. The flower heads are pale pink and thistle-like. They appear as a cluster on a stem which elongates to about 50cm, spreading them apart and usually twisting.

42 Grafham and Wintershall

About 8.0 km/5 miles with two extensions, both of 950m/²/₃ mile. Undulating farmland and woods on the Lower Greensand; bluebells in season.
OS maps 1:25000 145 +134, 1:50000 186 Aldershot.

Start from Rushett Common, TQ 022 423; park in one of the lay-bys beside Run Common Road near the A281 junction.

From the layby follow Run Common Road away away from the A281 past the houses and pond L. ◐

(e) *Extension of 950m/²/₃ mile: After the pond (100m) take the 2nd track L (200m). Cross the old* Horsham Railway *bridge and corkscrew down L under it to the Downs Link path. Stay ahead (SE) on the DL under a road (500m) up to the disjointed cross path (450m).*

(f) *Turn R through the trees (150m) and keep on along the L edge of the field to the end (200m). Join Whipley Manor drive (20m L). Follow it up R through Whipley Manor Farm (450m)* ✳ *to the main road, A281 (100m). Cross to the minor road opposite and follow it past Goose Green Farmhouse R (350m).* ➔(4)

(1) After the pond (250m), at the track from the farm L, turn R on the first path into the field. Follow the L edge (400m) and go on between gardens to the main road (100m).

② Go L along the pavement past ₃rafham Church (100m) and on up he slope beside the A281(250m).

③ At the top cross to the drives and take the L one (70m). Go past he house into the field and round he R edge to the corner (150m). Continue through the trees (150m) and ½R down the next field to the curving edge 50m before the R corner (150m). Cross the end of he next field into the trees (50m) and follow the track to the road in front of Goose Green Farmhouse 150m). ✳ Turn R.

④ Before the next house R, cross Goose Green ½L (100m) and turn L into the trees to the field (100m). Cross to the re-entrant corner and keep on L of the hedge (100m), over the footbridge and up the R edge of the next field to the tarmac drive of Tilsey Farm (300m).

⑤ Turn R passing a pond L. Stay ahead between barns (200m), on the gravel track with a hedge L 120m), over the rise and down to the bend at the trees (350m).

⑥ Keep to the main track round he pond past the house (100m). Stay ahead on the minor track in he scrub. When it bends L (80m) enter the field R and go straight up, aiming for the middle of the top edge (200m). Pass through the gap to the next field and L up to the adjacent field (30m). Follow the R edge out to Nore Lane, a major rack between fields (150m). ❖ ↘

Ⓧ *Extension of 950m/⅔ mile: Turn L up the sunken track (130m). At the bend climb the stepped path R. Turn R and follow the edge of he field up to the side path R between fields on the ridge (700m).*

Ⓨ *Turn R up the path between hedges or in the R field ↘ (Gatwick 25 km/15 miles E)(150m). Keep on through the wood, down past a major side track (400m) to the T-junction (200m).* ❸

Ⓩ *Go R (130m), down round the L bend to the road (200m). Turn R to the side path L (30m).* ➔⑨

⑦ Follow the track R over the rise and down to the road (700m).

⑧ Walk up the road L over the ridge and down past Scotsland Farm (300m) to the side path R 30m before the R bend (70m). ❸

⑨ Follow the side path (GW) round the edge L of the wood below the hillside (500m). On entering the field go straight on parallel with the top edge (200m) and down the track into the valley (60m).

⑩ At the R bend stay ahead, slightly R, up the steep path (60m). Cross the track to the grass and aim down ½R (see Wintershall, the large house R) past the corner of the garden to the drive (200m). Keep on along the drive, then the track to the road opposite Gatestreet Farm (450m). ✦✧

⑪ Turn R along the road (150m) and L at the next junction, to the next house (350m).

⑫ Turn R, next to the house, on the path to the fields (100m). Stay ahead from stile to stile (200m) and down the middle of the long field. There is usually no visible path. Pass close to the protruding trees at the R edge to the gate at the bottom, 50m from the R corner (400m). Stay ahead to the A281 (150m) and turn L to the side road (70m) for the parking place.

43 Shamley Green and Whipley

About 10 km/6¼ miles, extension 2 km/1¼ miles, short cut 1.6 km/1 mile.

OS 1:25000 145 Guildford + 134, Crawley, 1:50000 186 Aldershot.

Start from Shamley Green, parking in Woodhill Lane near the pond, TQ 032 438, or from the Run Common lay-by, TQ 032 419.

Linking walks
37✿ 38✿ 40✳ ㉜✦ ㉝✦

Bricklayers Arms ☎ 01483 898377
Red Lion ☎ 01483 892202

✦① From Shamley Green pond follow the road L of the green. Halfway to the main road bear L on the track. Watch out for the footpath between houses (100m). Follow it around bends to the field (200m) and up beside the hedge (150m). Turn R across the top of the field on the Greensand Way. Pass the church and cross the B2128 to the car park (450m).

② Turn L on the path near the road (150m). In the large field diverge R aiming for the nearest trees over the highest point. Go on along the edge of the wood to the track in the trees (450m).

③ Turn R (50m). Pass L of the house to the field (250m). Bear R to the cart bridge (100m). Cross the Bramley Wey and go on to the L bend near the house (300m). After the bend (50m) bear R to the Junction Canal. Keep on to the road and cross to the lay-by (200m). The wooded area is Run Common.

© Crown Copyright
MC 100011861

ⓢ *Short cut of 1.6 km/1 mile:* Take the path R of the canal at the edge of the field then through the wood (300m) and round R to the end of the pond (200m). Branch L over the DL path and go on through trees and along the field (400m). Join the Whipley Manor drive and keep on (R) to the farm (600m).→⑦

④ Take the path on the L bank of the canal to the fields (250m) and on (150m). Turn into the L field and diverge to the Bramley Wey. Follow the bank past East Whipley Farm (250m) and cross the cart bridge to the gate (50m). Turn R on the track through the fields (200m). At the concrete part go L round the bend then R, as before, to the next field (300m). Go up the L hedge (100m), and on as before to the side path R, 200m before the farm (300m).

ⓔ *Extension of 2.1 km/1⅓ miles: Stay ahead up to Rowly Farm (200m), between the houses and gardens and round the L edge of the field to the track (150m). Turn R to the next house (150m).*

ⓕ *Enter the field R and go down the L edges (200m). Cross the Downs Link path and keep on round L to the footbridge R (350m).*

ⓖ *Cross the Bramley Wey and continue between fields (200m). Turn L on the track (100m) and R on the side track. Stay ahead to the end of the long R field (300m).* ✳

ⓗ *Turn R on the side path (150m). When it enters the field, follow the hedge L to the farm drive (300m).*

ⓘ *Walk along the drive R to the next houses (350m) and continue on the lane to the A281 (500m).*

ⓙ *Turn R up the road (100m) and L up Tilsey Farm drive (250m).* ✿

ⓚ *Inside the farm gate, turn back R into the field and go down the L edge (300m). After the stream stay at the L hedge then cross the field slightly L into the trees (100m). Bear R across Goose Green (50m) and R along the road (70m).* →⑧

⑤ Go down the side path, over the Downs Link path (150m), over the Bramley Wey (100m), along the valley (150m), over the Junction Canal to the fields and up the track L then R of the hedge (600m).

⑥ At the top, go round the R bend to Whipley Manor Farm (450m).

⑦ Cross the A281 and walk along the minor road opposite (350m).

⑧ R of Goose Green Farm take the track into the trees (100m). Cross the R end the 1st field (50m). In the next, aim top middle (150m). Go through the wood (100m) and along the L edge past the house (150m).

⑨ Go down the drive L (70m), over the A281 and down to the pavement (100m). Carry on up past Grafham Church (150m) and on (100m).

⑩ Just after the Grange drive L, turn R on the narrow path through trees to the field (100m). Follow the R edge to the far end (400m).

⑪ Go L on the road (150m). Turn R on the next track, over the ex-Horsham Railway ✿ to the L bend (250m). Stay ahead near the edge, of the field down to the river (350m) and along the bank (100m). Cross. Continue up to the house (300m).

⑫ Diverge R from the drive (40m) and turn R on the path between fields, passing a farm track (350m) and rising to the B2128 (300m).

⑬ Cross the road. Turn L along the churchyard and join the road to Shamley Green crossroads (300m).

44 **Whipley and Smithbrook**

About 8.8 km/5½ miles. The two extensions of 1.3 km/¾ mile and 400m/¼ mile can be combined with the short cut of 2.6 km/1²⁄₃ miles. Undulating farmland. OS maps 1:25000 145 Guildford +134 Crawley, 1:50000 186 Aldershot.

Start at Smithbrook Kilns, TQ 026 392.

Linking 36✳ 38❀ 42✳ 43❊

Bricks Restaurant 01483 276780

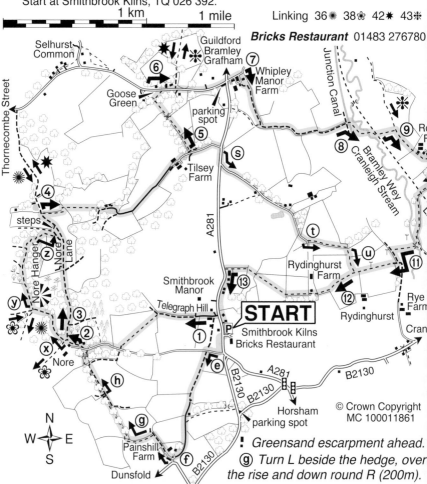

© Crown Copyright
MC 100011861

Greensand escarpment ahead.

ⓔ Extension 1.3 km/¾ mile: *From Smithbrook Kilns go L beside the A281 (100m). Just before the side road, take the lane R to the crossing byeway (120m). Go L to the house (450m) and on past it to Painshill Farm (350m).*

ⓕ *Turn R up the farm road past the barn. Continue on the track to the top corner of the field (220m).*

ⓖ *Turn L beside the hedge, over the rise and down round R (200m). Just before the corner turn R. The public footpath is between hedges. When it is impassable, go up the field at the R edge (300m).*

ⓗ *Turn R into the adjacent field and continue up the L edge. At the top, find the footpath between the fields. Go up into the wood and (N) down to the lane, joining it between drives (80m). Turn L (20m).*➜②

① From Smithbrook kilns go R beside the A281 (150m) and turn L up Telegraph Hill, the track at the drive of Manor Cottage (150m). Stay ahead on the farm track at the R edge of the fields to the start of the top field (250m) then cross ½L to the gate near the top L corner. The path is often invisible (350m). Carry on up the lane R, passing the drive of Pheasantry (250m).

② At the gateway of the house Nore, fork R up the rough track to the track junction (100m). ✳

Ⓧ *Extension of 400m along the hilltop: Turn L and R and carry on steeply up the hill to the cross path on the ridge (400m).* ↘↗

Ⓨ *Turn R up the ridge and keep to the R edge above Nore Hanger (450m). When the track bends L, drop off the end, winding downhill R (300m). Near the bottom go L on the cross track (50m) then R down the stepped path to the sunken track (150m).* Ⓩ *Turn L (100).* ➤④

③ Stay ahead on the track, Nore Lane, through the wood, past a track R from the field (500m) and over another rise ↘↗ (450m). ✳

④ At a dip, 20m before the pond, turn R through the field, R of the hedge (180m). At the corner, drop to the side field L (30m) and turn into the side field R. Cross slightly R to the protruding clump of trees before the house (200m). In the trees turn L to the house (80m). Go on round the pond (100m) and L up the main track. Stay ahead through Tilsey Farm along the drive to the gateway 80m after the barns and just after the pond R (700m).

Ⓢ Ⓣ Ⓤ *Short cut 2.6 km/1⅔ miles back to Smithbrook (on map).* ➤⑫

⑤ Just before the gate bear L into the field and go down the L edge (300m). After the stream stay beside the hedge then cross the field slightly L into the trees (100m). After the trees bear R to the end of Goose Green (50m). ✳

⑥ Continue on the road R to the A281 (400m). Cross and go into into Whipley Manor Farm (100m).

⑦ Turn R between the house and barn. Continue on the track which bends L&R and follows the L hedge (450m). Carry on round L and down through the fields R then L of the hedge to the Junction Canal (600m).

⑧ Cross the footbridge and follow the path R in the valley, over the Bramley Wey (150m) and up over the Downs Link path (50m). Stay ahead between fields (150m).

⑨ At the top turn R on the South Wey Path to Rowly Farm (200m). Pass between the houses and gardens then follow the edge round L to the track (200m). Turn R to the next house (150m).

⑩ Enter the field R and go down the L edge (200m). Cross the Downs Link path and carry on round L to the footbridge R (350m).

⑪ Cross the Bramley Wey and go on between fields (200m). Turn L to the path junction (100m) then R on the track. Stay ahead between fields, past a side path R (300m).

⑫ Continue round the top edge of the next field, L of the farmhouse (350m), and on beside the trees (150m). Cross the next field ½R to the corner (250m) then follow the stiles/gates to the road (150m).

⑬ Turn L. Follow the A281 to Smithbrook Kilns (400m). **Bricks Restaurant** is among the buildings.

The **A3** is the London to Portsmouth road of ancient importance. The old road from London Bridge passed through Kingston, Guildford, Godalming and other towns which were bypassed successively. The Hindhead bypass took the form of a tunnel, 1830m long, under Gibbet Hill which opened in 2011.

Albury is ELDEBERIE in Blackheath Hundred in the Domesday Book, held with many other manors by a Norman after the Conquest, Richard fitz Gilbert. It was rated at 2½ hides with a church and mill. The D'Abernons had it for 300 years. The medieval village was near the old church but in the 18th century the villagers were moved to the present site. Henry Drummond, a 19th century owner, built the present village church in 1842. Notable residents have been Malthus the political economist, Anthony Devis the painter and Martin Tupper the writer. The estate came to the Dukes of Northumberland through the marriage of Drummond's daughter.

Albury - a short guide to the parish 1998 24p

The **Amphibian & Reptile**Conservation Trust owns several areas of heath on Witley and Hankley Commons. Bare patches and log piles are for basking.

The **Atlantic Wall**, 100m west of the Lion's Mouth, was built by the Canadian Army in WWII for practice attacks.*www*

Barrows are burial mounds. In our area, all are Bronze Age bowl barrows from about 2200-1100 BC. Most have ring-ditches detectable if excavated. They spead over most of Europe from the end of the Neolithic. Early ones had beaker culture burials. Later ones had cremated remains in urns. Barrows are often in prominent places, possibly territorial boundaries. Many will have been lost to the plough and to erosion. All have been plundered.

Barnett Hill, the house, was built about 1905 in Queen Anne style by a London businessman, Frank Cook. His widow gave it to the Red Cross in 1944. It had been used as a convalescent hospital and became the national training centre and archive. It is now a country hotel.

Begley Farm was the home of Thomas de Beggelegh in 1332 according to the earliest subsidy roll. Bacga was an Anglo-Saxon man's name so *Bacga's clearing* is a likely origin of the name.

Binscombe has several old houses and the air of an ancient settlement. It was one of the tithings of Godalming. House-building has joined it to Farncombe and has brought to light much broken pottery of the Roman period. *Bin* may derive from bean-growing.

Blackheath was the Domesday Book hundred made up of Bramley, Shalford, Chilworth, Shere, etc. The men of the hundred probably met and held courts in the open on the heath. The village lies in the midst of the Common, which is presently 108 hectares, managed by Waverley BC for recreation and conservation. The Canadian army enclosed it as a camp in World War II which ended the grazing. It was used for army training during the Napoleonic wars and in Victorian times.

Bramley was a great Saxon estate of 34 hides. It probably included Dunsfold, Hascombe, Alfold and Cranleigh. The Domesday Book has no other places between BRVNLEI and the Sussex border and lists three churches. William the Conqueror awarded it to his half brother Odo, the Bishop of Bayeux. A railway platform is retained with fervour despite the absence of rails and trains. Bramley Mill is a 17th century building which operated until 1935. The church, Holy Trinity, is probably on the site of one of the Domesday Book churches but the nave is Victorian. The aisles are almost as large as the nave. The oldest fabric, probably Norman, is the west door arch (inside the porch).
The chancel dates from around 1210.

Bramley & Grafham Bramley Village Soc 1977

The **Bramley Wey** aka Cranleigh Water is a small river in an immense valley, best viewed from the hills on either side. It is aligned with the notch in the North Downs at Guilford which suggests it was the ancestral Wey. It flows from Vachery Pond and joins the present main Wey at Shalford.

Catteshall Manor house was the head-quarters of the Pitman organisation 1952-96. It appears to be a Victorian house but has a 17th century core and much older remnants. Henry I detached Catteshall from the large royal manor of Godalming for a retainer Dyvus Purcell.

Catteshall Mill was one of the three Godalming Domesday Book mills. It was part of a grant to Reading Abbey in 1141. Its earliest recorded uses were for fulling and flour. The rent in 1509 was 43 shillings and 10 sticks of eels! By 1661 it was a paper mill and in 1885 one of the earliest to use wood pulp. A sales poster of 1906 says it produced 30 tons of paper per week. In 1869 the wheels were replaced by a Fournyron turbine which last rotated in 1960 and was the largest known (37 kW); there is a model of it in Godalming museum. Catteshall lock is next to the mill.

Catteshall Mill Alan & Glenys Crocker
Surrey Arch Soc Research Vol 8 1981 64p

Chantries Hill is a Greensand ridge with thin seams of Bargate stone which give greater fertility and permits grass instead of heath in the Five Fields. It was given to Holy Trinity, Guildford in 1486 by Henry Norbrigge (mayor, d.1512; there is a brass plate to him near George Abbott's tomb). The rent or produce of a chantry paid the church for prayers for the soul of the donor or others. Often it funded a curate and school with pupils to chant the prayers. Chantries were dissolved soon after the monasteries by Acts of 1545 & 1547.

Chiddingfold is a nuclear village with church, inn and pond clustered beside a village green and with the old houses round it. *The Crown* may be the oldest inn in England founded as a Cistercian rest house of 1285. The first reference to the present site is in 1383. Edward VI visited and his retinue camped on the green in 1552. Despite evident antiquity Chiddingfold is not in the Domesday Book, its tax then being lumped with Godalming's. The earliest reference is to Chedelingefelt in a charter of about 1130. It became a market town in 1300 by charter of Edward I when it was the main centre of glass production and part of the iron making area. About 40 glassworks sites have been found locally, ten in the parish. Ancient church accounts elsewhere show orders for Chiddingfold glass. The village church, St Mary, has lancet windows, pillars and chancel arch in Early English style dating from soon after 1200. The nave roof was raised on extended pillars around 1450. The lych gate with its coffin table and Horsham slab roof was added in 1888 and restored in 1980.

Chiddingfold - the village & history of the Parish Church of St Mary H R H White 1999 44p

Chilworth is CELEORDE, in the Domesday Book, a small manor with mill held by Bishop Odo of Bayeux. The present manor house is 17th century, rebuilt by Vincent Randyll, owner of the manor and gunpowder mills, 1653-73, who sold up to the Duchess of Marlborough after the South Sea Bubble.

Chinthurst Hill was bought by Surrey County Council as public open space in 1961 to forestall building. The tower is a folly built in 1936 when the Chinthurst estate was part of Lord Inchcape's property. An ancient boundary mound on the hill is close to the modern Waverley/Guildford border. The eponymous house, 1895, was Lutyen's first large commission. It is now apartments.

Compton is CONTONE in the Domesday Book, a manor of 11 hides after the Conquest. Brixi was the tenant before that. It had a Roman house. In King John's time it was split into the five manors of Down (north of the Hogs Back), Polsted, Westbury, Eastbury and Field Place, each at present represented by a large house of the same name. The *Harrow Inn* has been licensed since at least 1780. White Hart Cottage is a 15th century house; it was a pub before 1780 and may have been the medieval church ale house. The church, St Nicholas, has a Saxon tower. The nave walls were replaced by hard chalk pillars when the aisles were added about 1160. The Norman doorway (inside the porch), font, lozenge mural over the chancel arch and coloured glass in the east window are all 12th century work. The chapel above the sanctuary is very unusual and its wooden rail exceedingly old. A graffito of a crusader is scratched on the south side of the chancel arch with a re-scratch cross, suggesting he got back. *The History of Compton in Surrey* Lady C Boston Compton PC 1987 247p

Cosford Mill has the oldest machinery in Surrey. Part of the building is 15th century. It closed in the 1890s. The wheel was taken for the iron in WWII.

Cutt Mill is mentioned in a medieval document in 1273 when it was given in a marriage settlement by John le Cotte to John le Paumer. The mill functioned until the 1930s but the only the pillars and shed in front of the house remain. The present house is the mill cottage. The millpond would be medieval in origin but The Tarn and the ladder of ponds a mile up the valley are Repton's work of the 1800s when he landscaped Hampton Park.

The Devils Punch Bowl is a large combe in the side of Gibbet Hill. The name does not appear until Rocque's Map of the County of Surrey of 1765, probably Georgian romanticism. Early names are Highcombe and Haccombe. Hegcumbe in a charter of 909 probably derives from hay growing in the fields where the bottom has been cut down to the Atherfield Clay. The clay raises the water table into the sides. Springs sap the Hythe sands which are largely unlithified but the sides remain steep because of low rainfall area and the sand causing absorption rather than run-off. Seams of stones stabilise the higher parts and were dug out of the slopes. The grey stones are seen in the cottages, originally for broom-squires.

Dunsfold is not in the Domesday Book probably then being part of the large manor of Bramley. It is Duntesfold in a 1241 assize roll - the earliest record. *Dunt* was a Saxon man's name. *Fold*, Saxon *falod*, implies a place of sheep folding, for winter. In spring shepherds would have led them along moltways to the heaths. The area has the greatest concentration of *fold* names in Britain. Dunfold grew into an industrial parish fed by local charcoal. Forges were still operating in 1653. Later owners were Richard Wyatt of Shackleford and Lord Montague. The church, St Mary & All the Saints, is almost in its original form of around 1260-1320 when Early English was becoming Decorated. In Victorian times the chancel arch was raised, the east window truncated and the west window rebuilt. Points of interest: the cruciform plan unusual for a small village church, ancient pews, three plug holes for floor washing visible outside (one in the west wall) and the elaborate sedilia.

Dunsfold airfield assembled jet fighters until 2001. It was constructed in 20 weeks in 1942 by Canadian Army Engineers for a Royal Canadian Air Force base in the build up to D-Day. It started with Mustangs, which shot up trains in France, and went on to have Mitchell bombers. After the war in 1946 it was loaned to Skyways Ltd whose Skymasters and Dakotas made 2749 flights in the Berlin Airlift,1948-49. Hawker took over in 1951 for testing prototypes and assembling the Sea Hawk, Hunter, Folland Gnat, Hawk and Harrier. In recent times the televison series *Top Gear* has been made there. *Dunsfold, Surrey's most secret airfield* Paul McCue 1992 Air Research Publications 297p

Eashing is ÆSCENGUM in the will of Alfred the Great, drafted around 885, a bequest to his nephew Ædhelm. It is Escingum in the Burhal Hidage, written about 915, listing the site of the buhr for the Wessex army. The 13th century Eashing bridges of Bargate Sandstone are similar to the Wey bridges at Tilford, Waverley, Elstead and Unsted, usually attributed to the monks of Waverley. Lower Eashing was a farming hamlet. Tankards, built about 1700, may have been a farm manager's house. The office block, half on the island, replaced

Eashing Mill in 1998, probably one of the three mills of Domesday Book Godalming. It was a corn mill in 1658 when converted into Surrey's second

aper mill. New owners modernised it
n 1852 to produce rolls of newsprint.
By 1865 it had 98 workers and made 10
ons of paper per week for The Times
and other newspapers. Latterly it was a
ock mill then an engineering works.

The 900year history of Eashing Mill
Alan Crocker Surrey Advertiser www

Elstead would have existed at the time
of the Domesday Book but it is not
sted because its tax data was part of
he great manor of Farnham's. The
ame first appears in the founding
charter of Waverley Abbey in 1128 in
which two acres at HELESTED were
onated by the Bishop of Winchester.
Elstead Bridge in Bargate is a 13th
entury bridge attributed to the monks
of Waverley, concealed in later repairs.
The second lane was built during World
War II. Old houses of the village are the
16th century Peace Haven & Lilac Cot-
age in Milford Road, Old Farmhouse
n Farnham Road and Domford on
hursley Road. The forge at the green
ates from 1686. Polshott Manor was
he Stovold family farm for 400 years
om the 15th century but has not been
working farm since 1920. Brookside
tarted as a small 16th century cottage
ut grew. Peter Sellers and Ringo Starr
ived there. The church, St James, was
chapel of Farnham by 1291 but parts
of the building suggest construction in
id-12th century. Built of chalk and
argate, the 14th century parts still
sible are the blocked doorway in the
hancel, the pointed chancel arch and
he middle window in the north wall.

Elstead then and now Gillian Drew 2001 81p

Elstead Mill is now a restaurant with
he wheel still in place. The building
ates from about 1800. It is probably
n the site of one of the six Domesday
ook mills of Farnham. It was making
orsted fringes when it ceased working
n 1881. In the 17th century it had been
orn, malt and fulling mills. A previous
ill was built in 1648. The mill rent was
0s 3d in 1208 in the Bishop's pipe roll.

Imley Farmhouse is a National Trust
oliday cottage. *Imbeleg* occurs in an
ssize Roll of 1255.

Enton was part of the Rectory manor
of Godalming owned by Flambard. He
was the chief adviser of William Rufus
but lost his land when the fatal arrow
brought brother Henry to power. Enton
Hall is now apartments. Enton Mill has
a date stone for 1621. It ceased milling
in 1899 and was turned into a country
house with Tudor features in 1908.

Frillinghurst takes it name from the
Manor of Fridinghurst & Ashurst whose
earliest court records date from 1550.
One of its manor houses may have
stood within the moat at South Park
Farm. The manor was hived off from
Witley and later absorbed back into it.

The **Ford Farm** fish ponds are used for
producing trout to stock angling ponds
on the Albury estate.

Frowsbury is a Bronze Age barrow. A
plaque indicates Queen Victoria visited
July 1858 to review troops on exercise.
Puttenham Golf Club opened in 1894.

Gatwick is a fairly common name from
the Saxon for goat place or farm. It is
consistent with the surrounding heath.

Gibbet Hill, 272m/895', is the second
highest hill in Surrey. It is *Kate's Knap*
on Senex's 1729 map of Surrey. The
trig point was one of the primary series
erected in 1936 for the 3rd triangulation
of Britain which began that year. Most
trig points are now redundant but this
one has been retained as a reference
point for GPS. The track on the north
brow of the hill, now under tarmac, was
the ancient London-Portsmouth road.
The shelf below was for its successor
which became the A3 in 1923. This
went into the Hindhead Tunnel in 2011.
The sailor's stone, 100m down the old
road, marks where the body of the
murdered sailor was found in 1786.

Gill is a Wealden word for a cleft with
a stream (ghyll in Cumbria). On the
Weald Clay, small flow produces large
V-shaped clefts, difficult to bridge.

Godalming Hundred appears as a
bequest in the will of Alfred the Great,
drafted around 885. The charter for a
market was given by Edward I in 1300.
Borough status was granted by Queen

Elizabeth I in 1574 and held until 1974 when the town was subsumed into the Borough of Waverley. The coat-of-arms has a woolsack. This was a medieval centre of sheep-rearing, weaving, fulling and dyeing, with power provided by the Rivers Wey and Ock. High Street was the London road to Portsmouth with coaching inns like the *Kings Arms;* Peter the Great stayed there in 1698. The *Red Lion* public bar was the old Godalming Grammar School. Prisoners on the way for transportation were incarcerated there. The Pepperpot is the old townhall which replaced the medieval Hundred House (court and office) in 1814. The first electric street lighting in the world was here in 1881. The generator was Westbrook Mill which was a leather works, probably on the site of a Domesday Book mill. Westbrokesmyll appears in the leet records of 1483. The church, SS Peter & Paul, was restored by Gilbert Scott in 1879. It is a large medieval church built on the original Saxon walls with some 9th century carved stones. The lead sheathed spire is 14th century.

Godalming - a Short History John Janaway 77p
The Brilliant Ray Francis Haverton Godalming Centenary Celebration Committee 1981 18p

The **Godalming Navigation** reached Godalming in 1763, extending the Wey Navigation from Guildford. It is lengths of improved river bed with cuts, rising 10m/32 feet from Guildford. It has locks at Millmead, St Catherine's, Unsted and Catteshall. The wharfs closed in 1925. In 1968 the commissioners gave it to Guildford Corporation who off-loaded it to the National Trust who now designate it as part of the Wey Navigations.

London's Lost Route to the Sea P A L Vine David & Charles 1973 267p

Gosden Common was the venue for a cricket match reported in the *Reading Mercury* in 1745 which appears to be the first known women's match; there is a plaque on the pavilion. The Bramley maidens scored 119 notches and the Hambleton maidens, 127; lbw may have been a problem. Gosden House, now a school, was the home of Osbert Sitwell's grandmother.

Grafham comes to light as an estate sold by Waverley Abbey around 1238. A later owner was Henry Woodyer, the architect, who built the church, St Andrews, in 1864 when the parish was created out of Bramley and Dunsfold.

Grayswood is not in the Domesday Book being then part of the manor of Witley. The earliest mention is for 1230 as Grasewode in the Loseley papers. The village is almost contiguous with Haslemere. The church, All Saints, was consecrated in 1902 and Grayswood parish was put together from Thursley Chiddingfold, Witley and Haslemere.

Great Tangley Manor house is a fine moated Tudor house but only the roof and gables can be seen from outside. The timber-framed façade has 1582 incised on it. Curved decorative braces are characteristic of eastern England. The Tangley estate was cut out of Bramley in the 13th century. This part became *Great* in the 17th century when the land was further subdivided.

GW, the **Greensand Way** is a 110 mile path from Haslemere, Surrey to Hamstreet, Kent, inaugurated in 1980.

Greyfriars Vineyard has open days. It started as a 1½ acre plot in 1989 on south facing Chalk, growing Pinot Noir and Chardonnay grapes. From 2011 the vineyard expanded and specialised in the production of sparking wines. It had 80,000 vines in 2016.

Hambledon is HAMELDONE in the Domesday Book a manor rated at 5 hides with a mill. The present church was erected in 1846 but has memorials from earlier churches. Documents show there was a church by 1291. Court Farm, the 17th century house next door, was the Manor House which held Courts Leet and Courts Baron. The kiln opposite the church was for chalk lime for making mortar. The *Merry Harriers* is an 18th century house. It was the subject of a famous Victorian painting: *A Country Inn* of 1862 (Tate). Myles Birket Foster, 1825-95, was a wood engraver, book-illustrator and painter at the start of colour printing.